I STILL HAVE MORE QUESTIONS THAN ANSWERS

An accidental journey through discipleship, life and leadership

Matt Hyam

WIPF & STOCK · Eugene, Oregon

Wipf and Stock Publishers
199 W 8th Ave, Suite 3
Eugene, OR 97401

I Still Have More Questions Than Answers
An Accidental Journey Through Discipleship, Life and Leadership
By Hyam, Matt
Copyright©2004 by Hyam, Matt
ISBN 13: 978-1-5326-5274-5
Publication date 3/8/2018
Previously published by Vineyard International Publishing, 2004

This book is dedicated to the memory of
Nicky Lennard
(25 July 1970 – 23 January 2004)

You were one of the five who started this church.
You and Jim were the first to get married.
You and Jim were the first to have children.
You are the first to finish your race.

Thank you, Lord, for the time
we were able to share with Nicky.

Contents

Acknowledgements	7
Introduction	9
SECTION I – REFLECTING	
1 Accidentally Starting Something	15
2 Becoming Respectable	29
3 What Was That All About Then?	37
SECTION II – RETHINKING	
4 What Is Discipleship?	53
5 Whose Lifestyle?	63
6 What About the Poor?	79
7 Worship	93
8 Leading, Serving and Toilet Cleaning	107
SECTION III – REDESIGNING	
9 Messing Up the Church	123
10 Rebuilding the Church	135
Books I Have Found Helpful	161

ACKNOWLEDGEMENTS

I would like to extend my sincere thanks to the following people:

my wife, Di, for your patient endurance of me as a husband and constantly clearing up the mess I leave behind – you are the best thing that has ever happened to me!

Todd Hunter, Duncan House and Pamela Evans for trudging through various drafts of this book and giving me support, encouragement and advice.

Sarah T for your incredible patience in reading through and looking for all my mistakes – honestly, it was teh kyeboard, not me!

Mark Stafford, for trudging through the first draft too and for being such a great friend and sounding board as we travel around the world on a chicken leg!

Dominic for lending me Claire's laptop, and Claire for not demanding it back.

John and Ele Mumford, for continuing to believe in us and giving us room to question.

Chris and Fliss Lane for taking such a huge risk with a group of weirdos who were playing at church.

My mum and dad for your backing and blessing – you have no idea how much that has meant to me.

Everyone at Southampton Vineyard Church. Being part of this church and being a co-worker with you has been the greatest privilege of my life.

INTRODUCTION

Most of what has become this book was written while my wife Di and I were on sabbatical for two months in Zimbabwe and South Africa. I never intended to write a book – well, maybe I did, but I did not really believe it! All I really wanted to do was to sit down and think through the last ten years during which we have been leading what has become – for better or worse – Southampton Vineyard Church.

I was twenty-three years old when we started this church, which means that I have been doing this for almost a third of my life – gulp! So much has happened in this time. There have been some great times and some really hard times. There have been times when I loved this job more than anything else and times when I thought that almost anything else would be better than this.

I wanted to be able to process it all. I wanted to write down my thoughts and my questions, my hurts and my joys. I wanted to be able to draw together the main points of the journey that we have been on during this time. I felt as though I was ready to burst and it had to come out somehow. I spent a lot of time sitting on the beach in Cape Town, feverishly scribbling down thoughts. As I wrote it all down, I found myself being challenged and revisiting questions I had tried to hide from but that had remained in the background, nagging at me.

The more I scribbled, the more I wondered whether anything that has happened to us might be of interest or benefit to anyone else. I began to wonder whether there might be a book in it. I do not presume to have any new ideas – in fact, I am very nervous of people who profess to have new ideas. I certainly do not think that our church is on the "cutting edge" (wherever that is). Any time that I do think this, I meet someone who has been following Jesus for longer than I have been alive and I see devotion and love in them that we have not even touched on and I realise how far behind the cutting edge we are.

Our church is not the best church in the world – frankly, often I cannot believe that people have stuck with it! There are so many other churches that are much better at making disciples, serving the poor, that have more impact in their community, that pray more, and that are more like Jesus than we are. But I love our church and most of the time I think that if I could be part of any church in the world, it would be this one.

I am not the best pastor in the world. Often when I meet other pastors, I feel as though, in comparison, I am a fraud. I am not a great preacher. I am not a great theologian. I am not great at praying. I am not a great leader. Actually, I regularly have to ask what I am doing in this job and how I get away with it!

It bears saying again: I do not have anything new to say. This may be the point at which you put the book down and find one that does have something new to say. Much of what I have thought through in this book is not original but has come from better men and women than I, who have influenced me, challenged, me and shaped my thinking. These people include John Wimber, John and Ele Mumford and, more recently, Todd Hunter, Stuart Murray Williams, Dallas Willard and NT Wright.

All that I have done is to piece together my understanding,

Introduction

interpretation and outworking of this, in an attempt to build a picture of what I understand it means to follow Jesus and, consequently, what this has meant for us to be church. What I have written is my account of our journey. These are my convictions, formed over my time as part of and leading this small community. I hope that in bringing all this together we can make sense of it.

The second half of the journey has been a process of rethinking my assumptions. This has caused me to question an awful lot of what I took for granted. This is a healthy thing for all of us to do – even if we come to the same conclusions that we started with. In my case, this process has led to a lot of change in my understanding, in my lifestyle and in the way that I lead this church. I have a far stronger faith than I ever had before and I am more in love with Jesus than at any other time in my life.

Much of this book deals with this process of rethinking and its implications. This is not because I want to be controversial or confrontational but because I genuinely believe that there are some really serious questions that need to be asked about church and discipleship. Often, in this book, I will open up subjects and leave them hanging. This is not because I think that I can deal with big subjects in a single page, but because I want to provoke people to look into them for themselves.

If I achieve only one thing in this book, may it be that people go away from it to look closely at the Bible without the assumptions they had before, and see where it leads them. I have included a list of some of the books that I have found helpful in this process as signposts along the way.

I Still Have More Questions Than Answers

I know that a lot is being made of postmodernism and Generation X, but I am not that sure that I understand what these things are or what they mean to the church. There was a time when I thought that I did, but now I know that I do not! What I do know is that I want to be an authentic follower of Jesus and that this desire has forced me into facing up to some uncomfortable issues and making some uncomfortable changes in my life and in our church. This is not so much a case of changing the way that we do things to reach a culture, but wondering whether what I had been sold was authentic in the first place. This process has been very destabilising in many ways and what will result is not necessarily cool or trendy, but I am convinced that it is necessary.

I do not have *the* model or *the* programme or even *the* answer to how to be more like Jesus. In many ways I am less certain than I was before. But I am becoming more and more sure that this is a healthy thing. I cannot put together a set of rules anymore. I am forced to seek what it really means to trust Jesus on a day-to-day – actually a minute-to-minute – basis. It has forced me to spend more time with him, to begin to know him more, to learn more about his ways, and I have to say that I love it!

I still have more questions than answers, but I trust that some of my questions will excite you too.

Section I

REFLECTING

1

ACCIDENTALLY STARTING SOMETHING

Lessons in humility

"In your humility God will give you authority." I just remember that line. There was more; something about being in a place of desperation and not success. I wish that I could remember the whole "word". Anyway, I was nineteen, had just started university, doing a course with a 100% employment rate, and this is what my youth minister prophesied over me at my baptism.

I remember chuckling to myself at the time. Why? Firstly, I was not humble at all – I think I even knew that at the time, which is scary, because evidently I did not do very much about it! I think back to what I was like and I cannot believe it. If I met the me from that time now, we would certainly not get on! Now, of course, as I frequently joke, I am *fantastically* humble. I had started university with the express aim of leading the Christian Union within a year. I thank God that he did not let me do that. I do not even want to think about what that could have meant.

Reflecting

I had only been a Christian for a year and doubt whether I had the necessary wisdom, experience and godliness that at the time seemed a given. God was pretty "lucky" to have me on his side. I should say at this point that I have met Christians who have been following Christ for a year who really do have the necessary character to lead; I was just not one of them – not by any stretch of the imagination.

So, there was the humility issue. Secondly, I had everything going for me – why would I need God's help? I was not sure about this whole idea of being in some way humbled so that I needed God. As I looked at my bright and shining future at university and beyond, I had nothing to worry about. It was clear to me that God would want me, his golden boy, to be successful, prosperous and happy. In the light of all of this, I just filed it away in the "wacky youth minister not hearing from God properly" file.

Off I went, knowing everything, a super-spiritual, future Christian superstar with God undoubtedly very pleased with me. Everything was very black and white – next to me, zebras looked rainbow coloured. I had no time for "sinners" and spent my time looking down at their "pitiful" behaviour and "irrelevant" lives. Obviously, I would speak to these "lesser" beings, but only for the sake of "evangelising" them, and I would make sure that I cleansed myself thoroughly afterwards. I had no real friends who were not Christians and I was generally not someone you would want to know. Nevertheless I was a great man of God, untainted by any of the sins that I did not like.

Just thinking about what I was like makes me cringe. It also makes me very nervous about what I will think in ten years of the person that I am now.

Accidentally Starting Something

It was in that time that God began to teach me what it means to be a follower of Christ. Despite all my diligence and hard work – well, okay, because of the lack of my presence at any lectures or production of coursework – I failed my first year at university and was sent home with my tail between my legs. Clearly this was a mistake on God's part, but what could I do about it? This was not the plan! I had failed only one exam and had the opportunity to resit it – an opportunity for God to redeem himself! Forgetting to bring your calculator to an engineering exam is a bad start and I would love to say it was the reason I failed. However, it was not. My resit mark was significantly worse than my original mark.

I began to wonder whether it was entirely God's fault or whether I might have had some responsibility in the matter. Suddenly, my world had crumbled around me. I was jobless, prospectless, humiliated and stuck in Luton. Things were not looking good. At this point I began to say sorry to God. He had given me an opportunity and I had failed to make any effort to take it. I had lost it.

Why would anyone do this?

My youth minister in Luton was starting a twenties group and I was asked to be one of the leaders. Aha! At last someone had seen my true godliness and value. Maybe things were not looking so bad after all.

From very early on I had wanted to be a leader. Not, I am afraid, because I wanted to serve the body of Christ, but because of a mile-wide ambitious streak that wanted recognition and prominence.

Reflecting

To my mind, I had been inexplicably overlooked when they had appointed care group leaders in my youth group and then the Christian Union had overlooked me when they had failed to appoint me as a Bible study group leader. What was going on?

But now, at last, here was my chance – a twenties group leader. Not just youth or the old "crumblies" but the *twenties* – surely the most important part of the church! With my super-spirituality, extra-vigilant legalism, amazing Biblical knowledge and new-found humility, there could be no one better to lead the twenties group. It was just a matter of time before I would be a nationally renowned leader and conference speaker (and rightly so!).

I would love to be able to say that leading this group was pure joy and a privilege that drew me closer to Jesus and enabled me to love and serve him in a truly special way. The only problem would be that that is not true. In fact, it was a nightmare pretty much from start to finish. The first problem was that the other leaders did not agree with me about everything – obviously God had not spoken to them or they were not listening. The second problem was the group themselves. They did not agree with me about everything either. What was the matter with all these people?

While I was obnoxious, bombastic, legalistic, arrogant and a number of other extremely unhelpful things, it was not actually all down to me. I can take the blame for a lot of it but not all of it. Two things have stuck in my mind from this time that really caused me to think about church and what it means to follow Christ.

The first was when I suggested that we all fast together, to which someone replied, "But we'll get hungry." There is not a lot you can say to that, is there (other than, "Yes you will")? That taught me a lot – just that one statement. I wonder whether there is an all-too-prevalent attitude of, "I will serve you, Jesus, in any way that you want as long as I am not inconvenienced in any way." Perhaps Jesus was only joking when he said that we need to die to ourselves in order to follow him.

The second instance was when we had a long conversation about bringing friends who were not Christians to meetings. All agreed that God was, indeed, in control of these meetings and very much present (whatever that means), but no one felt comfortable about bringing friends along unless we just had a social. (You would have to ask whether most Christians have shares in Nescafé from the number of coffee parties that took place when I was a new Christian.) Surely, if he is in control (maybe he was, maybe he was not, but the point is that everyone thought he was), we have nothing to fear? Why do we think that we cannot let anyone see what we really do? Do we trust God or not? Why do we need to organise socials – surely a group of friends would socialise anyway? Why do we not believe that God can reach our friends?

At this point I decided in my heart that I wanted those outside the church to be able to come to our meetings, see what we do and experience what we experience.

There were a few other high points of that year, most notably the youth minister's irrational blocking of my fantastic plan to take the whole twenties group on a beach mission (some lame justification for a holiday that is!). Okay, so we were going to go with Club 18–30, but they were much cheaper than anyone else. While I felt shackled by this heavy shepherding at the time,

Reflecting

looking back I would have to say that there might have been some wisdom in his decision.

At the end of that academic year, Southampton University graciously let me go back. And so it was that, with utter relief, I had to step down from leading the twenties group. I did so vowing that I would never, ever, under any circumstances, even consider the possibility of Christian leadership. Never! Whatever else I may be called to do, it certainly was not that. No way. No chance.

I once saw a Bestie cartoon on a greetings card of Moses with his arms spread in a dramatic gesture, parting the Red Sea. He is addressing the crowd of Israelites who have obviously just said something to him. His words, written on the caption underneath read, "What do you mean, 'It's a bit muddy'?" I rest my case!

How did I end up leading a church? The answer is still a little blurred. I will expand on the long answer in a moment. The short version is that, basically, I did absolutely everything that I could not to end up leading the little group we had started. God seemed to have other ideas. I am not the kind of person who will use language like "God spoke to me" very often, but on this occasion he really did speak to me about it very clearly. This was just after one of my plans to get someone else to do it had failed. I remember the words vividly, "I do not want you to shirk the responsibility that I have given you." There you have it. I gave up fighting at that point.

What on earth are we doing?

Do not ask me why we were not completely comfortable in any of the vast array of churches available to us, but we were not. Today I would seriously question any of the reasons I had then, but they seemed real to me at the time. I guess the easy answer would be that God made us dissatisfied, and that will do because it sounds the most "spiritual".

There we were – five of us. We were in the same church and we were close friends. Two of us had talked about starting a small group – a group of five of us meeting to sing, pray, minister to each other and read the Bible together. In the back of my mind I had always hoped that we would become a church – a Vineyard, more specifically. I loved the Vineyard style, I loved the music and I just wanted to be in a Vineyard church, but there was not one anywhere near us. It was a ridiculous idea fuelled, no doubt, by dubious motivations, and I never really thought anything would come of it.

There were a number of reasons for it to fail. Firstly, none of us had the slightest clue as to what we were actually doing; secondly, none of us had any idea of where we wanted it to go. Thirdly, all of us had different ideas as to what we wanted from it and fourthly, we had no leader, no experience, no vision, no plan and no direction.

Anyone who subscribes to established wisdom on church planting would, reasonably, be pulling his or her hair out at this point. We had no five-year plan. Actually, we had no five-minute plan! None of us had any track record. Well, not strictly true. There was my twenties group debacle and I had coordinated the music in the university Christian Union for 18 months – all of which clearly made me experienced. Then, there was Di (my girlfriend at the time and now my wife) who had led (very successfully) a Bible study group in her halls of residence in the university. There you have it; we were fully qualified after all.

Off we went. There were six of us at the first meeting, all crammed into my bedroom, with Di (our only experienced leader) not able to make it. We sang some songs and then discussed what we were actually going to do and when we were going to do it. I think that we decided to sing songs, pray for each other and study Joshua – why Joshua, I have no idea. We also decided to do it on Thursdays, which immediately ruled out one of the six. Good start! I think we may actually have looked at Joshua that night; certainly, we did once. It just never happened after that – there were too many other things going on.

Here we were, this ragtag group of friends, varying in how long we had known Jesus, how much we knew about him and how many times we had walked away from him. The one thing we did all have in common – apart from incompetence – was that we were really hungry for God. We would sing songs for ages, pray for each other until something happened and wait on God until he spoke to us. Often our meetings would go on until midnight.

Paradise Lodge

We very quickly moved from my bedroom to Paradise Lodge. Sounds good, doesn't it? Actually, it was a condemned terraced house in urgent need of renovation and was occupied (at least the three habitable rooms) by three of the five members of the group. It had, however, one redeeming feature – a very large

Accidentally Starting Something

upstairs bedroom that did not leak too badly (two buckets covered most of it).

We ended up being called the Paradise Lodge House Group. When we all went to New Wine, a large Christian conference held every year on an agricultural showground in the middle of nowhere in rural England, and had to have a name for the group, Di, who was handling the booking, had to come up with something quickly – so there it was. The people at New Wine assumed from the name that we must be an older persons group – an obvious mistake unless you had ever seen the house – and placed us on the outer edge of the campsite so that we would not be troubled by the noise. This was very thoughtful of them except that we were next to a generator.

The name did provide one last amusing incident when the first person moved to us from another church about a year after we had started. I asked her to write to the pastor of that church and ask him for his blessing for the move. It would seem that her handwriting was somewhat unclear because, in his reply, the pastor said that he was not sure that he would be able to bless her move to the "Parodic Lodge" until he knew more about it.

He was the pastor of the local Pioneer church. When I met up with him to explain the situation, he was more than helpful and affirming. On discovering what we were doing, his words were something like, "What can we do to help you get started? Is there anything that we can give you now?" He said that we were reaching people that no one else could and they just wanted to bless us. In fact, the leaders of other churches in Southampton were totally supportive of us from the outset, something that humbles me every time I think of it.

Reflecting

I am jumping ahead though.

We were meeting at Paradise Lodge. It has since been renovated and students live there now. I cannot understand why it was not left in that condition as a testimony to God's sense of humour! The funniest thing kept happening. We kept growing. We kept finding that disillusioned Christians, Christians who had walked away from Jesus and people on the fringes of churches began joining us. If we were ragtag before, we were even worse a few months later!

We felt God say two things. Firstly, we would be a watering hole and that people would come to be refreshed with us, and secondly that we would mop up the strays. I do not know if it was God or not, but both those things happened.

It was so much more than a once a week meeting. We were all friends. We lived with each other, we spent all our social time with each other – most of us were unemployed or students so we had a lot of social time!

I look back and laugh at some of the things that we did. I look back at some things and cringe. I look at other things and think, why did we stop doing that? Even as I write this, I am encouraged to see that we are still just a ragtag group of friends, just as incompetent, but trying to do the right thing. We may be bigger, we may have more cars and houses and pets, we may even have an office, but ultimately, we are still just struggling along trying to follow Jesus.

I remember the first time someone brought a friend who was not a Christian to one of our meetings. She ruined it! There we were being holy and enjoying God's presence (or is it presents,

I can never quite work out the theology of that!) and she was crying her eyes out. I am so ashamed to admit it, but I was so put out. I remember her crying and saying that she had never experienced love like this before and that she wanted to become a Christian. She had only come along to prove her housemate wrong. I had the meeting all planned that we would go from singing into praying for each other in a single movement of seamless grace. The atmosphere was great for that. I really did think (and very nearly said), "Why can't she go into the other room because she is ruining it for everyone else?" Oh God, oh God, have mercy on me!

My attitude was so centred on having this incredible experience with God that I could not see the lost or the poor, or anyone else but us! There were many good things that we did in those days but that particular aspect makes me very ashamed.

The Vineyard

All this time we were still, to one degree or another, involved in another church – the King's Church in Southampton. I rarely went to Sunday meetings now, six months into the life of this group, around April 1993. Through a process of elimination and God challenging me, I was leading the group by this time. Also, judging by the fact that he seemed to be taking us seriously and that we had more and more people involved with us – approximately fifteen at the time – it seemed likely that "it" was going somewhere – wherever that was! It was time to blow our cover. I remember being at a church meeting at the King's Church and realising that the time had come to speak to the pastor and tell him what was happening.

Reflecting

I approached him at the end of this meeting – very nervously, as you can imagine – and told him what we were doing. I will never get over the humility and godliness that Alan Baker showed that day. His first advice was that we needed to have some kind of "covering" or oversight. I told him that we were singing Vineyard songs and that our whole way of doing things was, as far as possible, Vineyard. He responded in a way I could never have expected. He advised me to go to the Vineyard and ask them if they would oversee us. He said that if they were not interested, he would look after us. What a godly man. Not a hint of him seeking to control us.

Someone actually seemed to believe in what we were doing. Maybe we needed to start believing in it ourselves.

I had been involved in St. Albans Vineyard during my final year at university – as involved as you can be when you live a hundred miles away. To be fair, I had been home in Luton and very close to St. Albans – much closer than anyone in St. Albans would want to admit – for three months and had got as far as housegroup the summer before we started our little group. I wrote to the pastor, Chris Lane, told him what was happening, what Alan had said and then plucked up the courage to ask him if he would "look after us". It was a shot in the dark. Our connection was dubious, to say the least, although Chris had told me that he considered me to be part of the church before I had left to go back to Southampton the previous September.

I remember him phoning our house in response while we were eating one night. You had to be careful answering the phone in our house because one of our friends had a tendency to call regularly, put on a funny voice and leave a false name. This was

Accidentally Starting Something

something that infuriated my housemates – particularly if they were the one caught out! Chris phoned and everyone assumed that it was this person. It was only when I spoke to him myself that I realised that it was for real. He did not dismiss the whole thing out of hand, which I saw as positive, and he invited me to go to St. Albans and talk to him.

I was so nervous! I was a little boy playing at church and here was a Vineyard pastor, one I had revered from afar, who heard every word that the Spirit of God said, who was clearly without sin, who actually knew John Wimber, the founder and leader of the Vineyard movement. On top of this, my dream of being part of the Vineyard was in his hands. I mean, this was the way in to the Vineyard – God's chosen people! (This is what it felt to me. Please forgive me for having been a horrendous, heretical and blasphemous fool!)

He started by telling me that he thought the whole idea was ridiculous, which was, perhaps, not exactly the start I was hoping for. However, he went on to say that he thought God was behind the whole thing and they wanted to adopt us as one of their "kinships" – that would be housegroups to us or cells if you are a trendy church. We were in the Vineyard! That was it! I could die happy now. What more could anyone want? We were in. We were part of the elite. Surely every Christian wanted this and we had it; and me, I was a Vineyard kinship leader and who cares that that sounds incredibly cheesy?

Chris went on to explain the deal. Basically it went something like this. St. Albans Vineyard would give us a box of Bibles, a load of teaching materials, support and an array of other stuff and, in return, they would come down and do some training

Reflecting

and teaching for us, and pay for us to go to some conferences. Now that is a good deal!

I did not so much drive back to Southampton as fly. I could not believe it! We were in! I was probably daydreaming about being a big, important Vineyard pastor with a big desk and a great building, walking around a big stage seeing everything that the Holy Spirit was doing, commanding demons to go in a really cool, understated voice any time that I wanted. Because that is what Vineyard pastors do. At least they do at conferences.

In those days I looked for every opportunity to pull out my Vineyard kinship leader trump card. I loved the status of being a leader and of being authenticated by the Vineyard. Today I do all that I can not to admit to being a leader when I am with other Christians. I try my best not to tell them I am a pastor because it seems that people treat you differently if they know.

The most amazing thing about being in the Vineyard was that, within our group, things did not really change at all on a day-to-day basis. To most of the group, being in the Vineyard did not really mean anything. We were definitely supported and encouraged, helped, trained and nurtured. From the point of view of the one leading the group, it really did change. However, I think that I had in my mind that as soon as we "planted the Vineyard flag", thousands would flock to us. I think I expected that owning the local franchise of such a credible movement would mean we would have a sudden influx of people. Weird how that did not happen! Thank God! Once again, I look back in shame as I realise that I had such an unhealthy set of expectations.

2

BECOMING RESPECTABLE

St. Albans Vineyard, Southampton Kinship

We were in. Now we could just sit back and watch the crowds pour in. I am very much ashamed to say that I was not at all concerned about the poor or those who did not know Jesus. All I was interested in was growing a big church. The two things should not have been mutually exclusive, but they were in my mind. I wonder whether I am alone in that kind of misguided motivation.

The next few years saw a lot of changes. We did grow, but slowly and mainly with the kind of people we already had – people who could not seem to find anywhere else. It was strange. I remember being frustrated that other Vineyards seemed to grow quickly – one of them had one hundred and eighty people at their first meeting! That is just not fair. It is not just that this is a competition (which obviously one would never admit) but it is the fact that my value is derived purely from the size of my church (which one would obviously never admit either). I am sure that I just imagine it but many of the conversations with

Reflecting

other pastors seem to include covert ways of asking how big each other's churches are.

Try as we might, we were still abnormal. We just could not seem to be like other churches – or even other Vineyards. It was probably two or three years before we had anyone in our church who was over twenty-five. It was not our plan. Ironically, at one stage we went out of our way to try to attract "adults", but it failed totally to the extent that those who were already hanging around tentatively seeing if they might fit into our church disappeared completely.

Being "too idealistic"

In the space of one week, two church leaders told me that, "You can't build a church with students." One of them told me this was because they were "too idealistic". How can you be too idealistic? Like Jesus, for example? Maybe you can become too hypocritical to follow through your ideals, but since when was subscribing to ideals a negative thing?

Because of the situation we were in, our people had few responsibilities, no mortgages, no money but lots of time for each other, lots of willingness to give whatever they did have and a real desire to do what was right. I maintain that these are the ideal people with whom to build a church. I would go so far as to suggest that if people learn to be generous when they have nothing, it is hard to knock that habit out of them later and it is more likely that they will be generous when they have a lot. If people start by valuing one another above meetings, they always will. It becomes part of their genetic code. If people who have nothing to lose have an attitude of doing whatever it takes to follow Christ, I reckon they stand a better chance of still being radical when they are relatively rich.

I remember when my old blue Marina estate car – "the Blue Streak" – finally died. I say mine but my dad would probably correct me on that because I "rescued" it from him one summer and never got around to returning it. After several false alarms, it finally died. One of my housemates stood up at one of our meetings and told the church that I needed a new car. Bear in mind that the church had no more than 20 people at this time, all of whom were either unemployed or students. Within a week, people had given £650 – from where I have no idea! The reason that it was so important was that my car was the only car. It was the van, the bus and the ambulance and everyone in the church was insured on it. Actually, there was one other car – a mini – and I will never forget the day that six passengers got out of it for a housegroup meeting. They had to get there somehow!

I look around on a Sunday morning now and I wonder if there are actually more cars in the car park than people in the meeting. It does make me a little sad but I am proud of our people because that generosity has, on the whole, continued. Last year, people in our church gave more than £70 000 to the poor and to various projects that we support in Southampton and in the developing world. This was on top of the normal, regular giving. We are not a big church – a little over a hundred "adults" in housegroups – and while we are, without doubt, middle class, we certainly have no wealthy people. I imagine the average salary in our church would be significantly below the national average. To me the people in our church are amazing and I like to boast about them!

Reflecting

I am not saying that we are the best church in the world. I am saying that we should not write people off as being too idealistic because they are not in middle management or in their forties. I am concerned that we ourselves have raised the bar and made it more difficult for students and younger people to lead – we have to keep checking ourselves. Do we allow people to make the mistakes we made? At the same time, I need to say that I think it would be just as much of a mistake to appoint young leaders – or any leaders – just for the sake of it!

Our housegroup reached twenty-five people, all of us crammed into a lounge. Boy, did it smell in there! You would be okay as long as you did not leave and come back inside because then the smell really hit you! We were fast approaching the point nobody wanted to reach. We were going to need to split our group. No one could bear to face it, but quite apart from the lack of physical space, we were actually having people come to our meetings who were not even being talked to. It was not that no one was interested in them. There were just too many people to notice everyone. It had to be done.

When the split actually happened, it was not nearly as bad as we had imagined it would be. We all still spoke to each other and, apart from a meeting once a week, things did not change that much. Once a month we all met together in a community centre for a meeting that was probably more like a normal church service than a housegroup.

Preaching

As things changed, so did my role. Suddenly we had these joint meetings and people expected me to "preach". I was terrified! I could not possibly do that. I was really not any good at it. Believe me, I am not being modest; I really was bad. It was bad enough having to speak at a housegroup meeting, which I could now just about get away with, but this was something entirely different.

I reached the point where I was trying to calculate how many meetings I really needed to speak at. At school I had been good at English except that my reading aloud was unbelievably bad. So bad, in fact, that everyone – including the teacher – thought that I was putting on an act to annoy her. I must confess that I did many things to annoy her and so I was very happy to allow everyone to think that this was just another of them. But it did not help me now!

I used to ask someone else to read any passages I was going to speak from. This would buy me a little time. I still needed to work out how to actually speak publicly. The next couple of years were a nightmare for me in that department as I tried everything I could to improve.

I listened to really good speakers who used no notes but were clearly totally in tune with the Holy Spirit. Naturally I thought that was the way to do it, so I would prepare nothing and just let the "Spirit speak through me". I can only conclude that he was not well on every occasion that I spoke because he was not very good at it, and he made me look stupid!

Then I would hear someone who wrote out the whole sermon word for word. How stupid of me; this way the Holy Sprit speaks to me first, I write it down, then I just read it! There were two problems with this. Firstly, as I have already mentioned, I am not very good at reading things, and secondly, the Holy

Spirit, once more, was not playing ball. Once again I looked stupid. This method was abandoned more quickly than the previous method because it was harder work and played to all of my weaknesses.

A further dilemma presented itself. Should I, in true charismatic style – and I believe we are meant to be charismatic – only talk on topics? Or should I, in true evangelical style – and I believe we are meant to be that too – expound the Word of God from a given passage?

It was all so confusing. I tried every combination and method that I saw anyone else using. The depressing thing was that they all sounded great when they spoke whereas I was becoming a very marketable cure for insomnia. Anyone who stuck around in our church in the early days deserves some kind of endurance award. Eventually I went to Chris Lane and asked him to pray for me, which he did. Things began to change.

I stopped trying to be like other people and began to be me. Basically, nowadays, I speak in public pretty much the way I speak normally to my friends – it is just me. Finding the style with which you are most comfortable is the key. I do not know if I am any better at preaching than I was before, but I enjoy it far more. It is just me chatting to my friends now.

Taking risks

Chris Lane really took a risk with us. Not many people are willing to take that kind of risk and I am eternally grateful that he was. For two years we were part of that church. Despite being a 100 miles away, they looked after us well. They gave us enough space to find out who we really were as a community, they let us make and learn from our mistakes and they were patient with us. Fortunately for us, Chris protected us from making horrendous mistakes. There were only a couple of occasions when Chris put a stop to my plans but he was always right and I never regretted submitting to him.

As someone who is prone to running around trying to do everything, I think the most significant piece of advice he gave me was this: It's a marathon, not a sprint. I have lost count of the number of times that I have quoted that.

We progressed from being the St. Albans Vineyard, Southampton Kinship to St. Albans Vineyard, Southampton Satellite Church when we had three housegroups and then, on 23 April 1995, we became Central Southampton Vineyard. Apparently Di and I were ordained on that day but we only found that out three years later! We are so religious! We have since dropped the "Central" on account of too many people confusing us with the railway station.

It has been, to use a cliché, a bit of a roller-coaster ride for everyone in the church, but I really believe it has been motivated by a genuine desire to do what is right. Every time God challenged us about something or we heard a new teaching or method, we would go for it. Consequently, there have been many changes of direction over the years. In fact, people dread me going off to conferences because they expect me to come back and change everything.

I am amazed that anyone has actually held on throughout the entire ride, but they have, and I really thank God for that. We are still muddling through, battling against respectability or, more to the point, battling against the desire to stop questioning ourselves.

3

WHAT WAS
THAT ALL ABOUT THEN?

During the existence of this little community, two major events have affected much of the church in the UK in one way or another. Many people will point out that both of these are still happening, but they affected us – and perhaps the church in the UK on the whole – for specific periods. The two events I am referring to are the Toronto Blessing, which hit us between May 1994 and Autumn 1995 and the Brownsville Revival in Pensacola which affected us from December 1996 until July 1997.

Both these seasons significantly affected us to the point of transforming our mission, our teaching, our goals, our meetings and, as a result, our community. Some of these things were positive, others seemingly less so. I realised that these phases were significant times in our history and yet we have never revisited them. For my own sanity, I realised that I needed to stop – albeit five years later – and reflect on how these events had affected us and, in a spirit of trying to understand and know more of Jesus and how he has worked in our church, to ask the question: What was that all about?

Reflecting

The Toronto Blessing

We were still a satellite church at the time of the Toronto Blessing. A team from St. Albans came down to take one of our meetings. I remember it very clearly. Tony Cooke, who was the assistant pastor at St. Albans Vineyard, now the senior pastor at Cheltenham Vineyard, was talking about a church called the Toronto Airport Vineyard. He had visited the South Yorks Vineyard, where a team had just come back from Toronto. He mentioned something about laughing and "things" happening to leaders when they were prayed for. You have to bear in mind that this was before anything had happened at Holy Trinity, Brompton and hardly anyone in the UK knew about this.

As he spoke about all this, I was thinking, "He's going to get me out there in front and then he's going to pray for me and I am supposed to fall about laughing." If anything ever looked like a set-up, this did. I made a definite decision that this was exactly what was not going to happen. The problem was that it did happen, the moment I was prayed for. Even my housemate and one of my closest friends, who was praying for me, thought that I was putting it on. I could not help it; I just collapsed in hysterics. There was absolutely nothing I could do to stop myself. Years later he was still convinced that I had been acting.

Several months of the same kind of thing followed. That meeting was in May 1994 and the strange manifestations, as they were referred to – people falling over, laughing, etc. – were still happening in January 1995. It reached the point that we stopped our housegroups and just had larger meetings at the community centre every week where people basically sang songs and then fell about laughing. We had loads of visitors during this time

What Was That All About Then

who came along to "get blessed".

In December 1994 I went to Toronto to experience first-hand what was happening there. I went with a group of six guys from three other churches. Apart from having a great time together, we all got "blasted", to use the technical term. On one occasion I was literally bouncing around like a pneumatic drill and ended up lying on the floor for an hour. When I arrived home from Canada and walked through the front door, my housemate's first words were, "You look so different."

Something was going on. There was a lot of teaching at the time centred around Ezekiel 47, which is very similar to the passage in Revelation 21, and talks about a river flowing out of the temple.

The last evening that we were in Toronto stuck in my mind so clearly. It was like a big party. Everyone was praying for each other and laughing and falling over and singing but two things kept nagging at me. The first was that, the more I read the passage they kept quoting, the more I saw the last line. The more I saw the last line, the more it seemed to be the whole point of the passage:

> All kinds of fruit trees will grow along both sides of the river. The leaves of these trees will never turn brown and fall, and there will always be fruit on their branches. There will be a new crop every month, without fail! For they are watered by the river flowing from the Temple. The fruit will be for food and the leaves for healing. (Ezekiel 47:12)

In the translation I read at the time, this reads "their leaves are for the *healing of the nations*".

Reflecting

The second thing that bothered me was that there was a young man in a wheelchair at the edge of the hall. I did not see anyone pray for him? Maybe he was too difficult? You could pray for anyone else and they would fall over or laugh, but what if he didn't stand up and walk? Surely that would ruin the party. I was as guilty as anyone else as I did not pray for him either – I am sure that I would have used the excuse that I was not part of the ministry team, but I am sure that, had I been, I would have had another excuse. My reason was the same as everyone else's.

As I walked out of the auditorium, I was haunted by this and cried out in my heart to God, "What is this whole Toronto Blessing for?" I looked back and I could see this guy – at last, someone was praying for him – and I felt God saying, very clearly, "It is for people like him." I took that to mean those that the Bible would call "the poor in spirit" – those looking for healing, the excluded, the broken, those society rejects, the oppressed and the broken, the suffering and those in poverty.

When the Toronto Blessing started in the UK, I heard that Clive Calver, then the director of the Evangelical Alliance, was asked what he thought of it. His reply was that, as long it resulted in the lost being saved and the poor being helped, he was happy. I, like perhaps others, took the attitude that he did not understand and that "God just wanted to bless his church". I am so ashamed that I even thought that. The Jesus in my Bible spent all his time with the poor and the oppressed. He made it very clear in Luke 4:18–19 that the essence of his mission was to serve these very people. He also made it clear that we would know something by its fruit (Luke 6:43). Therefore, if the Toronto Blessing or any other move of God was (or is) indeed a move of God, surely the fruit would be the lost being saved and the poor being helped.

What Was That All About Then

As I look back at how we were affected by Toronto, I have many questions. At the time I thought it was incredible and I never wanted things to return to "normal", but now I have to ask the question: Where is the fruit? It was more than eight years ago but I am not sure that I can see any fruit from that time in our church. Perhaps God did things deep in us that have been worked out over the years and we did not even know about it. Who can say?

I do know that nearly every book I read at the time – and there were many – defended and argued the biblical basis for the rather bizarre manifestations that were taking place, but very few that I could find talked about the fruit of what was happening. As far as I am concerned you can stand on your head whistling the national anthem of Tongo while barking and laughing and say it was the Holy Spirit, as long as when it is over you have been changed.

> But when the Holy Spirit controls our lives, he will produce this kind of fruit in us: love, joy, peace, patience, kindness, goodness, faithfulness, gentleness, and self-control. Here there is no conflict with the law. (Galatians 5:22–23)

Today, I would want to see the fruit of the Spirit and, specifically, a closer walk with Christ which I think would be shown by the things mentioned above and worked out by some element of Luke 4:18–19. If you have an apple tree, it cannot help but produce apples; it is the inevitable result of being an apple tree. If you have the Spirit of God living and working in you, you cannot help but produce the fruit of the Spirit. It stands to reason then, that if these qualities are not present, neither is the Spirit.

Reflecting

If the tree bears oranges, it is not an apple tree. That is not being legalistic, that is common sense.

Let us be careful of saying that things are "God" because they feel good or because everyone is doing them. I am not going to stop you doing bizarre things, but I am going to look for the fruit.

A number of things happened in our church as a result of Toronto. We stopped our housegroup meetings in favour of joint renewal-type meetings. The result was that the community of our church subtly began to break down. Those who were lonely were not being noticed and those who were struggling were not being helped. We became so focused on experiential meetings that we ceased to be focused on the rest of our lives. It probably took between six months and a year to get back to being a community again.

Three people came to a meetings one evening. They were absolutely stoned – on what, I have no idea. They came for no other reason than to mock us and to disrupt the meeting but, as it happened, things worked out very differently. Within minutes of arriving, one of them – a guy called Wade – was completely sober. He said later that it should have taken several hours for this to happen. By the end of the meeting, he wanted to give his life to Jesus.

We saw him the next week and he told us that, after that evening, he had spent the whole night sitting on his bed praying because he had "never thought about God before so he thought that he'd better get to know him". He told us that he had been a very angry person and that he hated everyone. Now he was a bit confused because he had not been able to hate anyone since it happened. That is pretty good fruit!

What Was That All About Then

He stuck around for a few weeks, was baptised and then we never saw him again. There were other stories like Wade's – dramatic conversions and people then vanishing without a trace – many of them with various outstanding arrest warrants and with different quantities of people's belongings which they "borrowed" and "forgot" to return. Maybe they are all walking closely with Jesus somewhere else. If so, then that is absolutely fantastic but I have to say that I am fairly dubious.

I really thought that the Toronto Blessing was a work of God. I loved it. I still have no problem with anything that happened in terms of manifestations, but I am desperately looking at our situation and struggling to find the fruit from it. You may have reaped incredible, lasting fruit in your setting. It may be that the lack in our case is due to the way that we pastored that period of renewal. Perhaps it was God, and we got it spectacularly wrong. I am prepared to believe that, but at the end of the day, I am left asking the question: What was that all about?

John Wimber, who eventually led the Vineyard to release the Toronto church, made the point that we should be very clear about what renewal is for: to get us back to our real focus, or what he called the 'main and the plain', which is reaching the lost, healing the sick and being with the poor. The tendency to elevate the phenomena and the tendency to focus on experience was unwise. He never questioned that God was moving or that the phenomena were of the Holy Spirit, but he did question how the renewal was being pastored, what focus was being given to it. Perhaps, if we had pastored what happened in our church better, we would have seen more fruit.

There was a lot of energy and excitement around, but we did not

Reflecting

channel it towards the priorities of the gospel. Now, as I reflect on that time, and ask these questions, it is not because I am against the gifts of the Holy Spirit or "power encounter". Over and over we have seen how God can work through the power of the Holy Spirit. I am just not sure that it all went where it was supposed to go, or that we pastored it in the best way.

The Brownsville Revival, Pensacola

A couple of years after Toronto, I started to hear about a place in Florida called Pensacola and a revival happening there. It excited me. Something in me thought there just had to be more to following Jesus than what I was seeing in my life and in the lives of those around me. I was hearing about a real fear of God, a call to be more like Christ and 100 000 conversions. I was scared, I do not mind telling you, because I knew what I was like and it was somewhat different from what Jesus is like.

Chris Lane had been to the Brownsville Revival and he really encouraged me to go. In March 1997 I went with three guys from the Community Church in Southampton, one of whom had been to Toronto with me. I was very prejudiced. It was very "Pentecostal", very "American", and all that I heard about it seemed very judgemental and legalistic. Come to think of it, I cannot think why I was interested in going! It did not take very long for me to be totally humbled, probably about ten minutes.

Our trip there was quite funny. On the first night I decided to lend my holy hands to the ministry team to pray for people and so I registered as a "visiting pastor". By the second night I was registering as someone who needed to repent of sin and turn back to God and, by the third night, I was not even sure whether

What Was That All About Then

I was a Christian and so I registered as a new Christian. Somewhere in their records there is the note of some idiot Englishman who came over as a pastor and gradually fell away and came back to God, all in the space of three days.

I was scared. No one was being judgemental. No one was being anything other than gracious, but God was showing me what I was like – and it was not nice. There was more to following Christ than I had been experiencing and I was aware of him challenging me. On the last morning we all looked at each other over our sugar-laced, health-free, all-natural-ingredients-removed cereal, and realised that all we were capable of doing was standing in the queue outside the Brownsville church building waiting for the meeting to start. This was about nine in the morning and the meeting started at seven in the evening.

I remember vividly standing in that queue feeling so convicted of my sin that I felt a weight on me that made it hard for me to breathe. I was literally struggling to stand up. At last, we were let in and eventually, when the altar call came, at the end of the meeting, all of us jumped over the seats in front of us and ran to the altar – or as near as we could get in the rush. We were desperate to be "right" with God. As I write this, I realise how absurd it sounds, and I suppose it was, but I was a very different person when I returned home.

It is hard not to compare Pensacola with Toronto, however unfair it may be, but two things leapt out at me. Firstly, in a week in Toronto, where the Airport Vineyard was the main tourist attraction in the city, we met only one person in the city who had even heard about what was happening. In a week in Pensacola, we literally met only one person who did not know

Reflecting

what was happening at Brownsville. The youth crime rate in Pensacola had dropped by about 13% in the year leading up to our visit whereas in Florida, as a whole, it had risen by 1%. The youth at the church were out every night talking to the street gangs about Jesus. Their leaders had tried to stop them because of the danger, but they just wanted to go. The Brownsville Revival was affecting the whole region whereas, at the time (and it may have changed now), the Toronto Blessing had not really had any noticeable effect in Toronto, apart from on tourism.

Then there were the manifestations – laughing, falling over, crying, and other generally weird behaviour – in both Toronto and Pensacola. In Toronto, there was book after book, explaining, justifying and interpreting them. In Pensacola, they simply said, "If you have a problem with it, then tough! What is important is that people are being changed." The emphasis was on lives being transformed. They wrote several books but almost all of them were about holiness, being more Christ-like and living obedient lifestyles.

I am sounding very pro-Brownsville Revival and very anti-Toronto Blessing, but I am not really. Both were among the most significant times of my life. I "enjoyed" Toronto a lot more than Pensacola, without a doubt. The Brownsville Revival left me feeling convicted, broken and terrified out of my wits by God. Something about what was happening really struck a chord with me and made sense. There had to be more to following Jesus than what I had known. If praying a prayer and then doing whatever you want is what it means to be "saved", why were there so many around me – myself included – whose lives did not look any different from their neighbours'? I did not like the style with which they did things in Pensacola, the idea of meetings being the focus, the suits and ties, or the thinking that the men at the front were more holy than the rest of us, but despite that, I loved it!

This is another reason why I have questioned how we pastored the Toronto phenomenon in our church. Cleary both Toronto and Brownsville were experiencing similar phenomena of the Spirit, but the focus was different. While the Pentecostal environment had some cultural things I did not relate to, on a deeper level the focus was more on the gospel and mission than on experience. They were taking it to the streets.

Having experienced two similar movements of the Spirit, not too far apart in time but with such different emphases, I can see that while we cannot cause God to move, we can certainly be responsible or irresponsible with what we make of it. I hope that next time, if I have the privilege of being around when there is a move of the Holy Spirit, my reflections will have made me wiser, and I will pastor what is happening with a clearer focus.

I came home excited about revival and preaching about revival. I heard prophecy after prophecy about revival. I heard prophecies, confirmed by other prophecies from all over the world about revival. I heard the prophecy about Princess Diana's death and the other prophecies that accompanied it about revival. I heard the stories of the signs of revival. I was looking for revival!

We prayed. We made ourselves ready. We prepared. We preached about sorting our lives out before God. We got scared. And we waited. We were doing all the right things. We had heard all the prophecies. It was coming. If you are a surfer – and believe me,

Reflecting

I am not – you know that the biggest, best wave in the entire world is irrelevant if you are not set up for it. But we were.

Several prophecies from all over the world indicated that revival was coming to the UK and would start on a specific date in May 1997. Amazingly, we had a day conference arranged for that very day, called Holy Fire. I am not usually one who just accepts prophecies but these were independent and all saying the same thing. There just had to be something in them. I really believed it. I fasted for ten days (okay, I was trying to fast for twenty-one days but had to abandon it halfway through) and I was excited! I even told everyone what I was expecting.

The night before the conference was really eerie. There was a strange atmosphere in the weather that I had never experienced before. My mother-in-law phoned us that evening and she commented that it was like "little fires burning everywhere", which was a very good description of what it felt like. It was really happening. We were really going to see revival starting at our conference. I was honestly expecting people to come in off the street and ask how to be saved.

The day came, and I was full of anticipation. About a hundred people showed up. It was a good conference and God really touched some people and I think he really changed some people. But no one came in off the street and no one got saved and revival did not start and, as far as I can tell writing six years later, it has still not. Not only that, Chelsea won the FA Cup that day. So overall, it was not a good day!

I was devastated. Not just about Chelsea, but about revival. I was broken and very disillusioned. It took a very long time for me not to treat all prophecy with extreme cynicism after that. To be honest, I still treat any prophecy about revival with extreme cynicism.

I fear that too many of us think that revival is God doing it all for us so that we are off the hook. He will feed the poor, he will speak to our friends and we can just sit back and enjoy it. I do not see any evidence that this is likely. A big part of me wonders what we are doing if we are not following him into his harvest field (Matthew 9:37–38; Luke 10:2,), setting the captives free (Luke 4:18–19), healing the sick, casting out demons and raising the dead (Matthew 10:5–8) and making disciples (Matthew 28:19). When the church, by which I mean each of us as opposed to the corporate entity that we call church, actually does this, that will be revival.

Where does that leave us?

I hear talk of revival and renewal and I hear prayers for revival and renewal. I hear speakers from all over the world advise on how to have revival. I hear stories about revival from abroad and in the UK. Sometimes I think, "Didn't I hear that same story, with the same statistics five years ago?" I hear a lot of Old Testament quoted (usually out of its context – especially 2 Chronicles 7:14) to back up the endless meetings and experts and events.

Maybe they are right and I am wrong, but where is the revival? Why are the poor not being looked after? Why is the church in the UK continuing to shrink across the board – house churches, charismatic churches, evangelical churches, and not, as we would love to think, just the traditional churches? Are we making disciples? Are we following Jesus in his mission (Luke 4:18–19),

Reflecting

or are we just hiding out in our Christian ghetto and waiting for it to happen?

If God does amazing things, I am totally up for it, but I will never forget hearing Jackie Pullinger talking at a Vineyard conference in Acton, in April 2000, called Doing the Stuff. She said that in Hong Kong, where she ministers to the drug addicts and prostitutes and some of the poorest people in the world, they heard about the laughter. She said that they heard about it and they waited. They heard that people got on planes and flew to the laughter and they waited. They heard about the laughter breaking out all over and they waited. They waited for people to bring the laughter to them. Surely, if God was giving his people laughter, they would bring the laughter to those who were mourning and weeping and desperate? But they never came. Why not? Very good question.

Back to that question again. What was that all about? In both cases – Toronto and Pensacola – I went full speed, dragging the unfortunate people of our church with me because I believed that this was the "big one". But it was not. Not only was it not "it", but it took months, if not years, to get back to the task in hand, making disciples.

Both things really felt like God but in both cases I truly struggle as I look around our church to see any fruit from either. I wonder if one day, in the age to come, I shall be sitting with Jesus over a cappuccino (and you can be sure that it will be fairly traded and have just the right amount of froth and espresso) and I will ask him what was happening. He will, no doubt, give me a blinding explanation and I will slap my forehead for being such a fool and not seeing it.

Section II

RETHINKING

4

WHAT IS DISCIPLESHIP?

Feeling your way around pachyderms

It was Autumn 1999 and I had gone back to Spurgeon's Bible College in London to finish my course, a part-time certificate in theology. This was partly because I did not like leaving things unfinished and partly because I thought that it was probably a good idea for a cowboy pastor like me, in a cowboy church like ours, to have some kind of theological qualification, for credibility if nothing else. I enjoyed the lectures and I quite enjoyed the study around them, although I will not dispute that I am lazy and rarely did more than the minimum required for me to pass. What I did not enjoy was getting up at five-thirty on a Tuesday morning and travelling for two and a half hours to get to East London. On more than one occasion I was suffering from "heavy duvet syndrome" and just did not make it.

The point is that I was really just there to attend, tick the boxes and get out. The last thing I expected was to be radically challenged about my faith or for my whole life to be changed. You just do not expect that from a Bible College. When I looked at

Rethinking

the timetable and saw that my first lecture was "mission", I imagined that it would be an old Baptist missionary rattling on about his time in some distant part of Africa and telling us that we should all go there. Not that I am at all influenced by stereotypes. I take my hat off to anyone who has devoted their life to serving God in isolated parts of the world, but I do object to the attitude that I occasionally hear, that if we are not serving God in the same way, we are not being faithful to him.

It was nothing like that. In fact, it could not have been less so. Stuart Murray (now Stuart Murray Williams) spent thirteen weeks dismantling many of the assumptions that I had about my faith, one by one. He challenged our Western interpretations of Scripture, discipleship and faith and presented alternative examples from the church and theologians from other cultures around the world. I had always assumed that no one would ever question these things. It had never occurred to me that our view was not the "pure" view or, God forbid, that it was actually less pure than others.

I love that *Calvin & Hobbes* cartoon where Calvin asks his dad why all old photographs are black and white. His dad replies that the photographs are, in fact, full colour but that the world was actually black and white in those days. I'm not yet a parent but I am really looking forward to that kind of power.

The world, in case you were in any doubt, is not black and white, and it never was. In fact, black and white films are more expensive to buy and develop than colour film. What is that about then? Someone, somewhere is having a laugh! The world is not black and white but, as an incredibly arrogant young Christian, my vision was entirely black and white. In fact there was no grey. As I have grown up and grown older, I have become increasingly aware of how much I do not know. My dad always used to say that the more you find out, the more you realise what you do not know. Obviously I just wrote this off as my dad waffling on, but he was right.

Do I believe in absolute, objective truth? Yes, I most certainly do. However, I have never met anyone – other than Jesus, if you want to be pedantic – with anything other than a subjective and biased view of that absolute, objective truth. I live in Southampton in the 21st century; Jesus lived in Palestine in the 1st century – see where this is going? That is just the starting point. All the assumptions of my culture have influenced my thinking and my interpretation of everything I see, hear and read.

It is like the three blind men feeling their way round the elephant – which, by the way, is not something to try yourself – and trying to describe it. One said that it was like a wall; another said that it was like a snake; the third that it was like a tree trunk. They were all correct, but they were also all wrong. An elephant is elephant shaped; that is the objective truth. We are the three blind men. Let us have the humility to admit it.

Christendom

The crucial, life-changing point came when Stuart taught a lecture on Christendom. This mainly involved looking at the changes that took place when the church went from being a small group on the fringes of Roman society – illegal, persecuted and radical in their discipleship – to being legal and powerful under Constantine, the emperor. Not only a legal organisation but one that required you to be part of it by law.

Rethinking

A number of agendas came into play here, but mainly the government and the church were well and truly in bed together. The radical, subversive Jesus of the New Testament that the church had followed for two hundred and fifty years really was not a great role model from the perspective of a government wanting to maintain control. On top of this, albeit a few hundred years before, the Roman Empire had actually had him killed and, clearly, it is a bit embarrassing for a Christian empire to admit to having killed the founder of their faith.

The emphasis shifted away from the man Jesus, focusing almost exclusively, on the "God" part of "fully man, fully God". This was much easier and in many ways far more convenient for the newly-formed Christian state. The Nicene Creed, for example, has almost nothing to say about Jesus' life; only that he was born, he died and he rose again. Did his life mean nothing: the miracles, his teaching, his lifestyle?

Slowly the goal of Christianity shifted from life to death. Jesus did not come to give us life but to enable us to go to heaven when we die. It would be hard for a ruling power not to be in favour of this. Jesus had nothing to do with the ruling authorities of his time except at his trial. In fact, most of what he taught about was how to be a marginalised people, living revolutionary lifestyles that will turn the world's values on their head. Most of his life the authorities – not without reason – were very nervous of him, his teachings and his lifestyle.

Jesus was a revolutionary. He did not teach us how to live in a Christian state because I do not think that was what he ever wanted. He taught us that we would be oppressed and persecuted because of him (Matthew 10:17). He taught us that the world would hate us because of him (Matthew 10:22; Mark 13:13; Luke 21:17). What we saw in the first centuries of the church was a persecuted, feared and mistrusted cult that was respected nonetheless by everyone because of their sacrificial lifestyle and the way that they helped those in need. Within less than one hundred years from the inception of Christendom, to its shame, the church had not only become respectable and rich, but had taken on the role of persecutor.

Instead of espousing radical living, under Christendom the church sent a message that was arguably the opposite of what Jesus taught. The need to govern necessitated the compromised gospel of, "If you are good (in other words, keep your head down and do not challenge the status quo), you will be okay." With that emphasis, who can question Karl Marx's assertion that religion is the opiate of the people? The sad thing is that Jesus hated religion as much as Marx did.

This is a very brief summary of what I heard Stuart teach and its impact on me. I recommend reading Stuart's book, *Post Christendom* because he does a far better job of teaching this than I can. Suffice it to say that this sudden realisation that we have inherited seventeen hundred years of agenda-driven thinking blew my world apart. Everything in me was excited by this, although I have to say that it has ruined my life and I truly hope I will never be the same again. It just seemed to ring true. It made a lot of sense to me to start to question things that I thought were written in stone, and to see that, in fact, much of what I had assumed is not what the Bible actually says at all.

Rethinking

What does it mean to believe?

The ground – the hard ground of my assumptions and prejudice – had been ploughed up. I was ready to hear a fresh view of biblical interpretation. Actually, that is not true. I was not interested in a fresh view so much as a better, less prejudiced view. This came about six months later when we went to Corona, California for a forum entitled Deconstructionists at Work led by Todd Hunter. Todd was the national director for the Association of Vineyard Churches, US at the time. The speakers were Stan Grenz, Brian McLaren and Dallas Willard.

I went, partly because we were, very generously, paid for by Vineyard Churches in the UK, partly because I do not like to miss out on anything and largely because it was Southern California in the summer. It was, to say the least, a strange time for us. We left five days after returning from India where we had been staying and ministering in an orphanage where everything was very simple. In India there are millions of people everywhere and it is smelly and noisy. Suddenly we were in Orange County where there are no people, only cars and cuboid buildings and everything is clinically clean and tidy and impersonal. It was quite a culture shock!

I remember looking at the reading list before we went. Frankly, I had trouble reading that let alone the books on it. I sat on the plane and tried to read the essential reading article. It might as well have been written in another language as far as I was concerned. Some of the conversations at the forum itself, however, made that article seem like an Enid Blyton novel. Di and I became increasingly aware that around us – these young leaders from the Vineyard in the United States – had Masters or PhDs in theology, and we felt very stupid.

Nevertheless, when Dallas Willard talked about atonement, he challenged my whole view of what it was all about. He questioned the standard evangelical view that, if we pray a prayer we can go to heaven when we die. It was like a seed being planted in my newly ploughed up ground. He challenged the idea that we have replaced "fact" (what the Bible actually says) with our "theories" about it. What does the Bible actually say about how to be saved? The Bible tells us that we need to believe in Jesus. What does that mean? What are we saved from? These questions have been the focus of my life and ministry since that day.

"Believing" in Jesus – *pistaeo* – means "putting all of our trust" in him. That is very different from our normal Western view of the word, which means giving mental assent to something. Believing cannot possibly mean a one-off prayer that does not actually change us. It must be about a permanent way of relating to Jesus, and therefore by definition it means that it has to affect every moment of every day of my life. It means trusting Jesus with my life. Jesus is fully God and the perfect human. Because he died and rose again, we can receive his wonderful grace and the gift of eternal life. We are not saved by our performance or our works of righteousness. But as the recipients of this wonderful gift, it must "work out" in our lives (Philippians 2:12). It is "by grace that we have been saved" (Ephesians 2:5), but this grace has "created us in Christ Jesus to do good works, which God prepared in advance for us to do" (Ephesians 2:10). If we never see the fruit, we must question if the grace has really been received. If we try to model our lives on Jesus in order to be saved, we attempt the impossible. But now that we are saved, he is the model of how to live. Trusting him means trusting that he knows best and living the way that he does. That has to affect everything.

Are we just saved from hell? Is it all just about what happens after we die? John 3:15 tells us that we will have "eternal life". What does that mean? We almost always read that as *"eternal life"*, i.e. life after death rather than *"life,* eternally". I am not sure that this is a good reading of this or a number of similar passages. The Greek word is *Zoë* and means "life in all its fullness". I think that a better reading of the passage would be "whoever puts all their trust in me will have *real* life, the way you were always created to live; and this will go on for ever".

I think that the emphasis of Jesus' life, message and ministry was that the kingdom – God's rule – was coming. His invitation was for us to live under God's rule now. In other words, to live the way that we were made to live. He never talked about, "going to heaven when we die"; he talked about living. Jesus came to save us from a wasted life that can only end on the great cosmic rubbish tip. The word used for hell is *Gehenna*, which was the name of the huge rubbish tip outside Jerusalem. All his hearers would have understood the implications of that. *Gehenna* was where all the waste and rubbish of the city ended up. He saves us from the life that ends up on the rubbish tip.

He offers us real life; life in the kingdom of God; a life of obedience to him. Obeying God is the way we were designed to live – it is the only way for us to be free from our addictions and the habits and patterns that are killing us. Salvation is not about trying to meet some criteria so that we are "in"; it is about living a life of obedience that is freedom and that life going on eternally.

What Is Discipleship?

I have heard Dallas Willard say on several occasions that we have created "a religion for death" whereas Jesus taught us how to have life – real life – in all its fullness. Gandhi said something very interesting: "If Christians were to live their lives to the fullest, there would not be one Hindu left in India."

God offers this life out of his grace. We can choose to take it or not. Taking it means living in the kingdom of God. To dejargonise this, it means to live under his rule – to obey him – because he knows how we are created to live and he can offer us freedom if we do. Choosing to obey, submit to and cooperate with God is to choose freedom – not a reward but the inevitable result. It is not legalism; it is just the way that it is. If you walk on a tightrope blindfolded, you need some guidance or you will fall off. To stray from the rope will result in a fall – it just will.

God has offered us salvation; that is freedom from a meaningless life, from a wasted life, from a life that we are not meant to live, from a life that is, literally, killing us. Alcoholics Anonymous offers a way out from alcohol addiction. It costs nothing, but you cannot be free and continue to live the way that you did before anymore than you can be rescued from drowning then jump straight back into the water. You have embarked on a hard journey that ultimately means you will be free but you must live differently to know that freedom. As I have heard Dallas Willard put it on a number of occasions, "Grace is not opposed to effort." In other words, we can never earn our salvation, but we need to make an effort to continue to walk in that freedom. "Hi, my name is Matt, I am a recovering sinner ..."

The crux of it is this: If I am totally honest, I realised three or four years ago that I was not really a disciple. Of course, I could raise my hands and close my eyes when we sang "You are the air I breathe", and I could feel warm and mushy at appropriate moments, but the truth is that he was not the air I breathed and if I were not a pastor at that time, I really do not know if I would still have been following Jesus. That is a shocking thing to say but the fact is that the only times that I prayed were for the church, the only times that I read my Bible were to teach from it and whenever we went on holiday and the pressure was off, I rarely even took my Bible and, if I did, it was not read. Somewhere along the line I had lost most, if not all of my relationship with Jesus and this went totally unnoticed and unchecked by me, if no one else. Something had to change.

Over the time since then I have been learning what it means to be a follower of Jesus all over again. I cannot cope without my Bible now – something is just missing if I have not read my Bible – and if I go a day without spending time with him, I really feel it. If I can change, anyone can. I really have changed as a person in this time – it has not always been easy and I am not perfect, but the more I have pursued following Jesus, the more I realise that "working out my salvation with fear and trembling" (Philippians 2:12) is going to take the rest of my life.

5

Whose Lifestyle?

If you put together a committee and asked them to take the beatitudes and create a religion that contradicted every one of them, you would come pretty close to what I am hearing down there at that church. Whereas Jesus said, "Blessed are the poor," down there they make it clear that it is the rich who are blessed.

… Jesus may have lifted up those who endured persecution because they dared to embrace a radical gospel, but that church espouses middle-class success and affirms a lifestyle marked by social prestige. (Tony Campolo, quoting a new convert on his view of a local church)

Blessed are the middle class

Perhaps reading this you, like me, have realised that the church referred to is not the only church like that in the world. If we are honest, there are very few churches in the West that are not like this. To our shame, we need to admit that something is just not right. As guilty as I feel reading this, I know there is far more of me in the description of that church than I would like to admit. The problem starts with me.

The aftermath of 11 September 2001 should give us some clues about the inherent problems with the values of our culture. One of the immediate effects of this horrendous event was that, throughout the Western world, if only for a brief moment, everyone had a glimpse of his or her own frailty and mortality. For a few days people flocked to churches to find solace, security and answers. For a few days we all realised that our world of comfort, convenience and entertainment was not as invulnerable as we thought. For a few days we caught a glimpse of what was really important in life – what really mattered.

For those few days, it seemed to me that being entertained did not matter much; the football scores were not so important; we did not need that new pair of jeans quite so urgently; that new television or DVD player, hi-fi, PlayStation, car or house just did not seem to be at the forefront of our minds as it was on 10 September 2001. Maybe it was my imagination, but it seemed as though, for a couple of days, people stopped buying things they did not need and stopped going through the motions of what is normal in the West. Stock markets became very nervous. Economies across the Western world began to slump. The system that we live under is totally dependent on us being consumers, and that means a lifestyle dedicated to buying things we do not need, doing things we do not need to do and living in a way we do not need to live.

The "success" of the entire Western world system is entirely dependent on one thing: greed. It is based on convincing us that we need something that, until now, we did not know existed, persuading us to buy it, and then, in a few years, months, weeks or days, convincing us that it is out of fashion and we need to replace it. If we bought only what we needed and lived as Jesus lived and taught us to live, the world economies would collapse!

Here is the frightening thing: I am really not sure whether I am more scared of the economy collapsing or facing Jesus and explaining my lifestyle to him. If the economy collapses, my shares will do badly and my pension will not be any good to me and ... and ... And what? And I will have to be dependent on Jesus?

It really worries me how addicted I am to this culture. I am so bound up in materialism and consumerism that I cannot see how much of it is actually completely at odds with Jesus' teaching. Do I really think that the poor are blessed – if I think about them at all – or is my plan to help the poor to enable them to become middle class? Do I actually think that being middle class is the goal of my faith? Because I have to admit that often I live as though that were true.

At our housegroup meeting one evening, I read the quote from Tony Campolo's book at the beginning of this chapter. I thought that it might make people think, we could all feel a bit guilty, repent, and then go home. I was, however, shocked to find that it provoked a discussion that went on for about an hour. In the end we had to curtail it as it was getting late. There were many things that came out of this talk that will, no doubt, take years to process but what struck us all was the realisation that we had assumed that we are somehow entitled to a comfortable, convenient, middle-class lifestyle.

Rethinking

What could it look like if we really took seriously what it means to die to ourselves (Romans 6)? What would it be like if I lived with Christ as my only reason for existence (Philippians 1:21)? What if I really learned how to love others the way Jesus does, to the point of suffering myself so that they would benefit? What would it be like if I lived in a way that was best for the planet and those who will follow after me, re-evaluating my lifestyle in the light of the environment? What would it be like if I sought to treat those whom I would never meet the way Jesus would treat them, and only bought from sources that did not exploit? What would it be like if I really shared my life, my money and my possessions with those in need, to the point that I would have to go without to do so?

Even writing this I feel uncomfortable because I know that I like my comfort too much. I know that to do this I will have to die to myself because it is just not possible otherwise. The way that I live affects other people whether I like it or not. My children and their children will inherit the damage I have done to God's creation. Families in the developing world go hungry because I want specific brands as cheap as I can get them, regardless of their employment rules or ethical values. Some things have to change!

The environment

I know that I have avoided looking into the environmental implications of how I live. This is probably because I know that what I will find will mean that I have to change things, and that is painful! Over recent months I have felt that I have run out of excuses and I have had to begin to examine the issues and make some changes in my lifestyle. It is annoying, in many respects more expensive and, most certainly, less convenient. But it is my belief that it has to be done.

Why does the issue of the environment have anything to do with us? Often I have heard the view that "it's all going to burn anyway" and so, effectively, we are excused from any responsibility towards environmental issues. The only problem with this argument is that it has no foundation in Scripture.

In the beginning humanity was given the task of looking after creation in partnership with God (Genesis 1:26–28). God saw his creation and it was excellent. We chose to reject God, and from that moment until his return, Scripture tells the story of the outworking of his plan to heal the world of the damage done to it. We need to be clear on this: God has not given up on his creation. He is not planning to destroy it but restore it. The idea of this "world" passing away, as translated in a number of places in the New Testament, would perhaps be more accurately translated as this "age" passing away. The word that is translated as "passing away" is a word to do with time – for example, the morning has passed away and now it is afternoon – rather than to do with destruction. In other words, this age will pass away and the new age – a term that has, sadly, been hijacked – where God rules fully, will come. This was the understanding of the Jewish people, Jesus' contemporaries and Jesus himself. NT Wright does far more justice explaining this in his book *The New Heavens and the New Earth* (see p. 164).

God appointed us as stewards of his creation. When we rejected this role, he set in motion his plan for the redemption of his creation. This plan would culminate in the final destruction of all that is evil and the restoration of the entire cosmos. His people would live in full relationship with God under his rule, no longer separated from him, able to walk and talk with him and know him fully. In other words, creation would be restored to what he originally intended it to be.

Where does that leave us? While the Bible does not speak specifically about "the environment", it is hard to ignore the whole thrust of Scripture. To do so would mean that we have to avoid some crucial questions. I have heard the argument that God is completely able to undo any damage that we do, which is undoubtedly true, so why does it matter what we do? My initial response would be to ask whether we are following Jesus and seeking to be his disciples, because if we are, we should be engaged in the same things as he is. If God is in the process of renewing this world, are we working with him or against him? If he is renewing and restoring his creation, should we not be doing the same? Certainly we should not be doing the opposite.

Our children, or our children's children, are in real danger of inheriting a rubbish dump with unbreathable air and no wildlife. It has already been said that there is no place anywhere on the planet that is not polluted. Would Jesus have taken part in the gradual destruction of the world? I don't think so.

Jesus' view on this is summed up in two statements he made:

> In everything, do to others what you would have them do to you, for this sums up the Law and the Prophets. (Matthew 7:12)

> "Love the Lord your God with all your heart and with all your soul and with all your mind." This is the first and greatest commandment. And the second is like it:

> "Love your neighbour as yourself." All the Law and the Prophets hang on these two commandments. (Matthew 22:37–40)

Looking after the environment is inconvenient. Disposable nappies are a lot less hassle than washable ones. Driving my car is a lot less hassle than walking, catching the train or cycling. Throwing everything in the bin is much easier than recycling. Even writing this manuscript we tried to use the back of scrap paper – what a pain that was. The bottom line is, however, so what if it is a hassle?

As long as we manage to think of the environment as merely an "entity" and not something that actually affects people, we can easily ignore it. The problem is that it does affect people, and it will even more in the future – real people, with real lives who do and will suffer because we cannot cope with a bit of inconvenience.

I am becoming increasingly aware that it is absolutely impossible to live the way our culture dictates and follow Jesus. The two are at odds with one another. Something has to give and the more I have thought about it, the more uncomfortable I feel. I have reached the frankly inconvenient conclusion that, if I believe that God is restoring this world and I am serving him, I have to pursue actively the good of the environment as part of being a disciple. Just because I believe it is what Jesus would do.

Ethical buying

Along with environmental issues, this has been a growing challenge to me over recent years. My wife and I changed our bank account recently because our bank could not give us any kind of ethical policy – they do not have one. We have started to rethink what we buy, where we buy it and how it affects others. Once you begin to scratch below the surface, this has to affect your life.

Would I give money to a slave trader? Would I give money to someone who is systematically oppressing, persecuting and violently treating people? Would I give money to an arms dealer? Would I give money to a company producing pornography? I sincerely hope that my answer to all of those questions is "no". But the reality is that while I am not actually putting the money into their hands directly, indirectly I do give money to those things. As long as I cannot see the person who is suffering, I am willing to ignore the problem. Would Jesus do that? I don't think so.

Is this a peripheral issue for a few extreme lefty, weirdo people to bang on about? The only real question to ask is: Who is my neighbour? Is my neighbour a slave in Africa? Is my neighbour a child labourer in India? Is my neighbour a victim of an oppressive regime on the other side of the world? If I believe that Jesus tells us to love our neighbour, I have to see ethical choices in buying and investing as a fundamental aspect of being a disciple.

If I want more stuff, then it needs to be cheap, but often a reason that it is cheap is because someone, somewhere is not getting paid enough, or even because of child or slave labour. I must start by questioning whether I actually need more stuff and then be willing to pay more for what I do need so that no one has to suffer to sustain my lifestyle.

At the time of writing, world coffee prices are, in real terms, the lowest they have been in one hundred years. In other words, the

Whose Lifestyle?

farmers in the developing world are paid so little for the coffee they produce that it is actually better for them not to harvest their crops. I want my favourite coffee. But that farmer and his family want to live.

Some years ago, a Channel Four documentary, *Slavery, A Global Investigation*, revealed that approximately forty percent of all cocoa imported into the West is produced by slaves. Not low-paid workers or child labourers but slaves. As children they are kidnapped or sold into slavery for the rest of their lives so that you and I can have Easter eggs. Not so long ago a ship was sighted off West Africa that was suspected of being full of child slaves. It was headline news for a time and we were all horrified. But I am still happy to eat the chocolate they are forced to produce for me.

What is the difference between me forcing a slave to work for me and buying from a man who does the forcing for me? We can now buy fairly traded chocolate, coffee and tea relatively easily, which guarantees fair pay to all involved. It is a bit more expensive, it is a bit harder to find than our normal brands and, to be honest, it is a little inconvenient. It is, like many things, a bit more of a hassle. But, we cannot allow ourselves to pretend that we are unaware of the suffering that is going on.

Is my financial prosperity dependent on the success of the pornography industry? Is my money being used to help oppressive and evil regimes? Presumably, none of us would knowingly invest in something we do not agree with, but if we do not choose to invest in ethical funds, it is possible. There could be less of a return on an ethical investment. I may end up with less in my pension fund, but that is a choice I need to make.

Rethinking

I would rather not know about this kind of stuff. When I did not know, I could be blissfully ignorant and stand before Jesus totally innocent. Even if I did not know, there would still be slaves making my chocolate, farmers kept in poverty making my coffee and children in sweatshops making my clothes. These are my neighbours and I should treat them as I would want to be treated. If I were a slave in Africa, I would not want people in the West to force me to work in inhumane conditions.

Money, materialism and radical living

Reading Acts 2 and 4 we see that in the church in Jerusalem, it was normal for people to sell everything and give all the money from the sale directly to the poor or to the church to distribute to the poor. I do not believe that we are commanded anywhere to give everything away in this manner. In Acts 16:14–15 we see Lydia who was "a maker of purple cloth" which, translated into today's culture, means a tailor to royalty – in other words, she was loaded – so loaded, in fact, that the church appears to have met in her house which, clearly, she had not sold. In 1 Timothy 6:17–19 we see Paul telling Timothy to tell the rich not to allow their money to become their security.

While giving away everything was relatively normal behaviour in the early church, the kind of radical lifestyle that characterised the early church is extremely rare in the church today. Why? I know maybe a handful of people in the church who have given away everything.

Do we assume that God wants us to have the best job, the best house, the best cars and the best standard of living? Where do

Whose Lifestyle?

we find that in the Bible? Jesus made himself lower than anyone has ever done. Paul tells us to imitate Jesus (Philippians 2). As we discussed this with our housegroup, I had to admit that for us, having only one car would be a sacrifice. How can having only one car be a sacrifice? There are people in the world who are starving to death and we think that owning two cars is our right.

I do not think it is wrong to own two cars. I do not think that it is wrong to be middle class. What bothers me is that this is our default setting. From what I read of Jesus' life and teaching and the early church, I see that the default setting was to leave everything behind and follow Jesus. How many people do you know who have done that? Not many, I would guess. There are usually one or two slightly crazy, radical people who have given up promising careers and futures to follow God, but they are the exception. What I cannot get away from is that this was one of the distinctive features of the teaching of Jesus and of the early church. While they had some rich among them, there were not many.

I have always assumed that I would have the best house and car I can afford, with all the trimmings. As long as I was reasonably generous, surely this is what God would want for me? Maybe I should turn that on its head. Maybe I should assume that God would want me to live as though I had nothing and give the rest away? Now there is an uncomfortable thought!

We live as if we think that God has given us this standard of living as a right and to give anything away is a sacrifice. Why is it our right? Who ever said that it was our money anyway? If your boss went away on a trip leaving you in charge and came back to find that you had spent the company's budget on yourself, there would be a problem. It is his money, not ours (1 Chronicles 29:14).

It is not wrong to live in a big house, but it is not your right, no matter how much you earn. God gave you the skills and opportunity to be able to do the job that pays that much. It is not wrong to own a big, new car but it is not your right. If God allows you to do these things, great, but just because you can does not mean that you should. Would you consider living on the bread line as your "right" and anything more than that as a blessing (1 Timothy 6:1–10)? How would that affect your idea of what sacrifice means?

Tragically, it seems that the higher the per capita income of a church, the less people actually give to the poor, to those in need around them or to the church. Why is that? I think that tithing is a cop-out to some and a crippling burden to others. Ten percent is not even noticeable to many of us, but to others it means they can barely afford to live. I think that God has called us to a radical lifestyle characterised by generosity and extravagant giving to those in need. There should be no needy among us. It is his money, after all. I recommend Stuart Murray's book, *Beyond Tithing*, for a more in-depth look at the subject of money. Suffice it to say that if you think that a ten percent standing order is your "job done" and the rest is for you, I am afraid that you may have missed the point.

He has called us to a life that will turn the world upside down, and that cannot start with my needs and God receiving the excess; it has to mean starting with him.

The richest people in the world

> I consider that our present sufferings are not worth comparing with the glory that will be revealed in us. (Romans 8:18, NIV)

I have always read this passage knowing that Paul's heart is so far from what I am like that I cannot conceive of it. I have begun to understand it, although I cannot claim that it is true for me yet. Here is a man who has been unjustly beaten several times, almost killed several times, repeatedly kicked out of various cities. What is the matter with him? Paul understands. He really knows what life is about:

> The apostles left the high council rejoicing that God had counted them worthy to suffer dishonour for the name of Jesus. (Acts 5:41)

Are they mad? They have just been left in prison overnight, sent to the kangaroo court where they have been unjustly accused and almost executed, and finally let off with just a flogging.

How could Betsie Ten Boom exude so much joy in the midst of a concentration camp that, even in death, people could see the ecstasy on her face? How can there be person after person in the persecuted church all over the world through history who has endured torture, beatings and imprisonment and come out full of praise for Jesus? What is the matter with these people?

In a culture where we equate happiness with success, material possessions or promising circumstances, the idea of anyone being happy in circumstances that are cruel, unjust and evil is alien to us. We read that Jesus will give us real life and we assume that means success, health and prosperity. Where does it say that? Where does Jesus demonstrate that in his life? We become annoyed with God when things go wrong. I know I do.

We recently bought a car. We prayed about it, we handed the whole thing to God and he seemed to give us a clear answer. Since we bought the car, however, we have had problems with it almost non-stop. I felt angry with God, I felt cheated by him, I felt disappointed with him. Why did he let us have this hassle? It is a car. We still have food, a home, we are healthy and, at the end of the day, it is just a little inconvenient. How on earth would I cope with being in prison for my faith when I cannot cope with a small technical problem?

When a team from our church first went to India to work with Pastor Samuel in Tamil Nadu, we spent five days living in one of his orphanages. There were 50 children from the ages of two to sixteen and ten widows living in the Erumad home. We slept on the floor and washed in buckets, which is not the normal way most of us live. It was hard to feel sorry for ourselves, however, when we realised that these children were sleeping three to a bunk, on boards, because we had their mattresses. These children eat meat once a week. We had meat every evening, and they had our leftovers.

These children were, without exception, the most godly, selfless, happy, satisfied people I had ever met. They had nothing, absolutely nothing, and yet all of us on the team knew that these children were so much richer than we are. They knew what it is really to live. Out of a team of sixteen people, every one of us prayed for at least one person who was healed, including a blind eye seeing and a paralysed person walking. We saw a

Whose Lifestyle?

number of people give their lives to Christ and were used by God in ways that stretched every one of us. However, if you spoke to any member of the team and asked what affected them most, they would tell you it was these children.

We came home ashamed of all the superfluous stuff we own and put our trust in. We came home stunned by the fact that we are, in reality, so poor. Jesus promises us life but we read this through our Western filter. I glimpsed the secret of life in those children. I began to see how Paul could be so full of joy in prison, how Peter and John could praise God for allowing them to suffer for him, how Betsie Ten Boom could be filled with joy in a concentration camp, and how countless believers throughout history could be martyred yet retain their joy until the very end.

Life has nothing to do with our circumstances. Life means that we are really alive, even if we have nothing. Life means that it does not matter whether we are in prison for our faith, permanently sick, on the streets begging or living luxuriously in a mansion. Real life has everything to do with being satisfied with knowing God. It has nothing to do with wealth, health or success. We saw that in these children. I have never met more alive people. I want the kind of life that they have. If we can learn to live like that, we will be free indeed. Here is the way to do it:

> So don't worry about having enough food or drink or clothing. Why be like the pagans who are so deeply concerned about these things? Your heavenly Father already knows all your needs, and he will give you all you need from day to day if you live for him and *make*

> *the Kingdom of God your primary concern.* So don't worry about tomorrow, for tomorrow will bring its own worries. Today's trouble is enough for today. (Matthew 6:31–34, my italic)

A better way of translating "kingdom of God" in today's language may be "rule of God", in other words, to make his rule your primary concern. This means to make being obedient to him your priority above anything else. This is the essence of what it means to believe or trust in Jesus. If we will believe that he knows best and we obey him, we will know life. If we insist on continuing to do it our way, worrying about material things, no matter how hard we strive, how much we own, how much status we have, how successful we are or how many holidays we go on each year, we will never really know life.

6

WHAT ABOUT THE POOR?

Who are the poor?

It all seems straightforward – minister to the poor. Well, maybe it is not so clear. Who are they? That may seem a strange question, but it is one that troubles me constantly. Is it obvious who the poor are? For that matter, is it important? Let me try to explain the issues that I struggle with.

When we go to India and see the work that Pastor Samuel (Sam) does in Tamil Nadu, it is very easy to see who the poor are. These children are orphans. One of the boys at the home in Coonoor, who was about two or three years old when we last saw him, was so desperate when they found him and his brother, that they had been eating gravel from the roadside. They had nothing else. All over India there are hundreds of children like him, begging on the streets just to be able to scrape together enough to continue existing. They really have nothing. They are utterly destitute.

In Jesus' time, to be a widow or an orphan meant that you had no means of supporting yourself and, without help, you would

Rethinking

die. In many places in the world today, like in India, this is still true. These people are obviously the poor. At the time of writing this, we have just spent five weeks in Zimbabwe working alongside people who work with orphans, nearly all of whom have AIDS. I actually found myself envying the church there because, for them, it is so clear who the poor are and how they can best be helped.

We live in the UK. We have a welfare system and a health service that, for all their faults, mean that no one is – or should be – starving on the streets. This itself breeds a certain culture among those on benefits. People who have only ever known the benefit system throughout their upbringing and adult lives have no expectation – or maybe even intention – of ever working. I often hear people talking about "getting paid" when they collect their benefit money.

Also, disturbingly, among a lot of people in this situation, everything is seen as their "right". I worked with the Dorcas project in Southampton, delivering free, second-hand furniture, bedding and beds to people who have very little and, in some cases, nothing at all. What I just could not believe was the attitude of the recipients. Obviously, no one does this kind of work in order to receive praise, but I can honestly say that in a year of working there, I could count on one hand the number of people who showed any kind of gratitude. In some cases they actually turned down items because the colour or the style was wrong! Many of these people had been referred by their social worker or health worker and saw this furniture delivery as their entitlement. They seemed unable to see that this furniture had been donated and delivered by people who wanted to help them because they were in need.

What About the Poor?

At the moment I play a very small part in helping to run an organisation that provides employment, training and skills to homeless, long-term unemployed people. These are people who are, to all intents and purposes, unemployable. This organisation exists to help them to become employable. The main criterion in selecting people is that they actually want to get out of the rut they are in. You would not believe how hard it is to find people who want this. Many do not show up for the interview; many do not show up for the job; most are consistently late or absent, and many have been sacked because they have walked out, over and over again. In the first year of doing this, we never managed to have a full quota of employees, because we just could not find enough people in all the hostels who actually want to help themselves!

These people are poor, without a doubt, but they do not sound the same as the poor Jesus talked about or ministered to. Maybe they are. We quickly end up with a concept of "deserving" poor and "undeserving" poor. Who am I to judge? How can I distinguish?

What about the person on the street selling the *Big Issue*? The government in the UK is very seriously looking at pulling the plug on the whole business. Why? Because, according to their research, it is not actually helping people get out from where they are. According to the government agency responsible for addressing homelessness, many of the vendors are still claiming benefits, thus committing benefit fraud, and using the money to support their drug habit. The problem is that while they are bringing in a very good income from benefits and from the *Big Issue*, there is no incentive for them to find a job. Finding a job would mean that they would no longer be able to claim and would actually mean a significant cut in money. Am I helping anyone if I buy the *Big Issue*? I just do not know. There are certainly some who are using it the way they are meant to. How do I know? If I do not buy it from this one, he or she may be one who really is trying. Have I just looked into the face of Jesus and refused to help him?

On the day that I wrote this, we arrived at Johannesburg airport, to be greeted in the lift by a well-dressed woman who begged us for money. She told us that she was a Christian like us and that she needed money for bus fare to Pretoria because she could not find work in Gauteng. Oh God, oh God! How do I know what the truth is? Airports are the perfect place for scams, so what should I do? We said no, but what if we had just looked into the face of Jesus and refused to help him?

A few years ago I met a guy on the street in Southampton, sitting in a doorway of a church building begging, so I took him to Burger King. I bought him lunch and we chatted. He was, I imagine, around twenty years old. He told me that he had always had work and that he hated begging and desperately wanted to work again. He told me that he had lost his last job when his boss took on a load of illegal immigrants, paying them very low wages, and sacked everyone else. He was, he told me, sleeping under a car wash at night. I asked him what he needed to be able get back on his feet. He told me that all he needed was a flat or bedsit so that he had an address. Once he had somewhere to live, he would be able to apply for a job and he would be fine. He told me that he was saving up a deposit from his begging.

What About the Poor?

It all sounded very plausible to me so I gave him eighty pounds for a deposit. In hindsight, I was a fool. I should have taken him to the housing office and paid them the deposit. I confess that the reason that I did not was that I did not want to use up any more time of my day off when I could be doing what I wanted to do. A lesson. In the days that followed, I phoned the housing office and sure enough, he had never gone there. A few months later I saw him begging in town again. I am pretty certain he never intended to pay a deposit or to find a job. I managed to get that one spectacularly wrong. What would you have done? He looked like Jesus to me.

This is a million miles away from a child in India or Zimbabwe or anywhere else in the developing world begging for food to live. Obviously there are many scams even in these countries. Often someone else controls these children and takes a large part, if not all of what they receive from begging, but even so, the children are absolutely dependent on begging. Certainly, we can support work in these countries financially from here but I just cannot believe that this is all Jesus wants for us. It just seems too distant and cold. It seems to cost us so little and, ultimately, it does not really affect our hearts that much. Please do not mishear me – I really think that we should be supporting work like this until it hurts and, as a church, that is exactly what we try to do, but I do not think that this is all we should be doing. We have to find our own poor – in England, in Southampton, and we have to learn how to serve Jesus by serving them.

Trying to serve the poor

About eight years ago, Duncan, the assistant pastor at our church, and I sat down and formulated a plan to begin to minister to the poor. Our long-term aim was to reach the point that, for everyone in the church, this was a normal part of his or her life. Our belief was then – and still is – that serving the poor is an integral part of being a follower of Christ and that we as a church should reach the point where it is actually happening among us. We realised that we would not be able to go from doing nothing – which, up to that point we had done very well – to everyone suddenly doing this off their own bat, in one step. We set ourselves a medium-term aim of having everyone in the church involved in some kind of existing project to do with the poor. Even this was too much for a first step and so our short-term aim was to find out what was already happening in the city and to piggyback it.

That was eight years ago and, to be honest, I am not sure how far we have moved from there. We have a reputation among the churches in the city of being a church that serves the poor. I am really not sure that this is a fair reputation. If it is, that is more of a sad indictment on the rest of the churches than anything else. Most of our housegroups have some involvement in projects with the poor. Most people in our church have a strong sense that the poor should be high on our agenda – they would have to, really, because I bang on about it so often! Many people in the church give generously to support local and international work with the poor. A lot of people in our church work with the poor for a living – social workers, psychiatric nurses, hostel workers, working with the homeless and the like. A few of the people in

What About the Poor?

our church really do minister to the poor as part and parcel of their lives. I wish that it were more, but then I look at my own life and realise how far I fall short in that respect and so I cannot wonder why the church does too.

We have deliberately moved away from setting up projects as a church, because we want people in the church to take responsibility themselves. We have invited several people from various Christian organisations in the city who are serving those in need to speak in order for people to have the opportunity to hear about what is happening and have the chance to get involved in the things that move them.

I remember John Wimber telling a story of a young man in his church who approached him at the end of a service one Sunday. Some weeks before this man had taken in a man from the streets and this man was now living in his home. He had phoned "the church" about sorting something out for the man but, after three weeks, nothing had been done and he was pretty annoyed about it. His question was, "When is the church going to do something about him?" I can imagine the mischievous grin that John would have had on his face when he replied, "It sounds as though the church is doing something already."

I think that it can be very easy for "the church" to organise a project and for individual members of the church to sit back, safe in the knowledge that they are serving the poor by proxy. I just do not think that this is what God has for us. We are the church, and if the church is not doing anything, it is because we are not doing anything; or, more specifically, it is because I am not doing anything.

Rethinking

Matthew 5:3 uses the phrase "blessed are the poor in Spirit" instead of "the poor" as in Luke 6:20. To be honest, I have heard this term used too often as an excuse and I would suggest that to focus on just these two passages does not do justice to the emphasis of Jesus' ministry to the poor and the marginalised.

I think the poor in spirit are those who do not fit. They are those no one else cares about – the lonely, the hopeless, the desperate, the outcasts and those no one notices. Many of these are materially poor; many are not. I wonder whether, by definition, these would be people whom we would have to go out of our way to associate with because they are not the people that we naturally hang out with. It will cost us to be Christ to them because the very thing that makes them poor in spirit will make them hard to be with. It is entirely possible that, in the world's terms, you may not receive much in return from the relationship.

I am not sure whether that makes things easier or harder. I am sure that we should still continue to provide food and clothing, help and shelter for those who are materially poor, even knowing that it may be a waste of time and money. Maybe that is what Jesus meant by the paradox: "Be as shrewd as snakes and as innocent as doves" (Matthew 10:16). We should always think the best and try to help even if we suspect we may well be taken for a ride.

How do we make disciples of the poor?

Jackie Pullinger described the King's Arms (a New Frontiers International church in Bedford) as the only church in the UK who were really ministering to the poor. Perhaps this was unfair given the assumptions that were involved but, nevertheless, they do a very, very good job and have done for many years. One of the leaders once told me that, in all the years that he had been there, he had only ever seen around half a dozen of those that they had helped become disciples. Contrast that with Pastor Sam's work in Tamil Nadu where all the children are following Christ, and I mean really following Christ to an extent that makes me feel like a fraud!

I do not know the answer. I have depressing story after depressing story and very few encouraging stories to balance them out. But we keep at it. We keep trying. I am convinced that relationship is the key. If I had not been so self-centred with the guy on the street, if I had invested time and not just money, things might have been different. Often, time costs us more than money. Valuing people means giving them time and building relationships. That is going to cost because the very nature of those we want to help means that we will receive very little in return.

I would like to be able to throw money at things and for that to be enough, but I am afraid it is not. I cannot see an option for doing nothing and so I firmly believe that each of us has an earnest responsibility to find out who the poor are, how we can help them and then do it! They may not be like the poor of Jesus' time but they are just as desperate.

Every month Social Services in Southampton circulates a catalogue of "unadoptable" children among its staff. Maybe they are too old – six, seven, eight or nine years old (people really want babies); maybe there are two or three siblings who need to be together; maybe they are just too difficult. Whatever the reason, no one wants to bring these children into their families.

Rethinking

Perhaps we – the people who are called the church – should adopt them. Perhaps we can give them a family. It will be very messy, without a shadow of a doubt, and our lives will never be the same again. But neither will theirs.

We live in a city that has a large number of asylum seekers. If these people are not the poor, I do not know who is! Many of them have escaped from horrendous situations that we can only begin to imagine in our wildest nightmares and they are desperate for help. We can offer them a meal at least, surely? We can offer them friendship. I was introduced to a Kurdish man. I say "man" but he is only seventeen. Two years ago, after escaping from Iraq, his parents climbed onto one truck in Turkey, and he climbed onto another. His truck came to England but he has no idea where his parents' truck went. He has not seen his parents since that day. All he wanted was to play table tennis with someone. So we played table tennis.

One day my wife met a prostitute outside her place of work. She needed the toilet, so Di invited her in to use their toilet rather than squatting in the corner of the car park. She told Di that she had been at university when she was nineteen but she became hooked on drugs and ended up in prostitution. She hated what she did so much that she had to get drunk just to go to work. She was living in a tent and she showed us her "home". We helped her to move a broken, rusty old caravan so that she could upgrade to sleeping in that instead. We bought her flowers for her new home. A couple of weeks later she was cleared off the land with everything that she had in the world – the contents of her tent. Can I see the face of Jesus in that poor woman who has to get drunk to do the work she needs to do to feed her addiction?

What About the Poor?

Our last church office was near a notorious bed and breakfast in Southampton. It had the reputation as the worst place in the whole city, but this was where most of the "hopeless" street people were placed. Most of these people were long-term homeless with serious drinking or drug problems. It seemed that the council turned a blind eye to the state of the place because to challenge it would mean having to find somewhere else for them to go. No one really cared about these people and they were better off the streets where no one could see them.

I met a man called Robbie. He was probably in his fifties. He was always drunk and always sitting or lying on the pavement outside our office. He lived in this B&B but had tried on several occasions to break into the disused building next to our office because that was a better choice for him than where he was currently living. Over time I began to get to know him better. One day, three guys from our church cleaned out his room for him. It took the three of them an entire afternoon to clean one room. You do not want to know what was in the sink or under the bed, but you would understand why a semi-derelict building was a better option.

We managed to persuade Robbie to go to the Salvation Army to come off the drink. He was doing okay but he managed to find ways of smuggling drink into his room and never quite managed to come off the drink. I do not know where he is now. Maybe he is clean. Maybe he is not. Maybe he is still alive. Maybe he is not.

None of these stories has a happy ending – yet. I can make myself seem very good at loving the poor but the truth is that, although there may be one or two more stories like this, they certainly do not characterise my life. What frustrates me is that they should. They should characterise all our lives because, frankly, if they did then it would have an impact on our nation like nothing else ever has, probably since John Wesley.

Perhaps it would be helpful for us to lose the idea of "helping" the poor. Henri Nouwen was asked about the sacrifice that he had made in living with a severely disabled man who was literally unable to do anything for himself. His reply is, perhaps, shocking to us. His reply was that he gained far more from the relationship than his friend ever could.

> Jesus gives us the opportunity to feed him by feeding those who are hungry, to clothe him by clothing those who are naked, to heal him by caring for those who are sick, and to offer him shelter by housing those who are homeless and unwanted. (Mother Teresa, *No Greater Love*)

Perhaps the poor are the elderly in a culture that values youth. Maybe they are the disabled. Maybe they are the prostitutes. Possibly they are the single parents. Possibly they are the asylum seekers and refugees. What about the older man who lives next door to us, who lives on his own and drinks himself to sleep every night, waiting to die? They are all around us and we need to do something before we have to explain to Jesus how we ignored these cries for help.

What About the Poor?

The old man who lives next door to us is called Maurie. Once, two years ago, he collapsed in the bath due to a combination of drugs his doctor had prescribed. It was three days before anyone found him, still sitting, barely conscious, in the bath.

When I first wrote this I did so because I felt God really challenging me about befriending Maurie. I came back from my sabbatical and I was a bit disorientated and it took me a while to readjust to life. Then I had to attend a pastors' conference, go to a forum in Washington and then I was a bit busy doing "holy" things. Then I went on holiday. Again, I felt that God spoke to me about Maurie. I came back from holiday and knew that I had to go and see him.

I made one attempt at seeing if I could do any shopping for him but I received no reply when I knocked at the door.

Three days later, I learned that Maurie was in hospital. He had collapsed at home with a tumour on his lung and a heart condition. Apparently, out of desperation, he had tried to smash the glass in his front door, just to try to alert someone – anyone – to the fact that he needed help.

That night Maurie died of heart failure.

Oh God, please have mercy on me!

7

Worship

> I hate all your show and pretence – the hypocrisy of your religious festivals and solemn assemblies. I will not accept your burnt offerings and grain offerings. I won't even notice all your choice peace offerings. Away with your hymns of praise! They are only noise to my ears. I will not listen to your music, no matter how lovely it is. Instead, I want to see a mighty flood of justice, a river of righteous living that will never run dry. (Amos 5:21–24)

I learned to play the guitar very soon after I became a Christian and my friend gave me his old guitar when he bought a new one. My mother will tell you how long she had to endure listening to me practising at home that first year. Very soon after starting, I ended up "leading worship" at the notorious twenties group I mentioned earlier, just because there was no one else to do it. We only ever sang about three different songs, either because the Holy Spirit only ever led us to these three or because they were the only three I knew. I am a little hazy on that one.

Over the years I have hungrily read just about everything that I could lay my hands on about worship, especially from the

Rethinking

Vineyard, and I loved it. I have trained worship teams and developed a philosophy of worship at my university, which is still running some ten years later. I have taught the Vineyard values of worship at national conferences, in churches in Southampton, in churches in other cities, in India and to anyone who would listen. I was sold on this thing. If you had asked me then, I would have said that I would rather lead worship than do anything else.

Some years ago, something changed in me and I found that I was getting, for want of another word, bored with singing songs. Something in me ceased to be satisfied by it. I could not get away from the fact that, as I looked around, I was becoming increasingly aware of people – and I include myself in this – who were singing songs with all their heart at meetings and yet living lifestyles that were not congruent with what they were singing. Something in me began to question how this could be right.

How could singing a few songs mean that we have "worshipped" when our lives tell another story? I would often lead worship and be lost in the experience when, in reality, I had not spent time with God all week and I certainly could not mean the words that I was singing. I am not sure that his name really was "honey on my lips", that he really was "more precious than silver", that "nothing compares to [him]" or any number of things that I sang with real feeling. I would sing them, but my life was far from the reality of them.

As I was reading through the Old Testament prophets, I began to see a pattern of God judging Israel because they had limited their worship to their gatherings, festivals and assemblies while neglecting the poor and the outcasts and addressing injustice. I think that God's opinion on this is very well, if alarmingly, summed up in the passage from Amos 5 quoted at the beginning of this chapter. It was this that disturbed me more than anything else, because it actually sounded like our church – or, dare I say, the church in the Western world.

I had always taught that worship is not just about singing songs but I was beginning to question whether what I really believed was that it was just about singing songs. Certainly, I had to admit that the way that I lived my life would back this up. I began to feel such dissatisfaction about this that I began to wonder whether the emphasis we, as a church, placed on worship – by which we really meant singing songs – had a precedent in the New Testament. The result was that I sat down and studied the New Testament to see what it does actually say.

I believe that, whatever our experience may be, we need to take seriously what the Bible says rather than build theology around our experience. What I found in the New Testament, as I sought to really study it, shocked me and was sufficient to turn my view through almost one hundred and eighty degrees.

What does the New Testament say about singing?

In New Testament times, in a culture where there was, obviously, no television or radio and where people were not literate, songs would have been a significant part of life. Families would sing together, stories would be told through song, lessons learned through song, fun would be had through song and spirits would be lifted through song.

I think that it is fair to say that, to some degree, songs were

Rethinking

clearly a part of church life. The church sang songs to each other and to God. In fact, in most of the references in the epistles, the exhortation is to sing to one another in the community of God and to others outside the church about God (Romans 15:7–11; 1 Corinthians 14:13–19; Ephesians 5:15–20; Colossians 3:15–17; James 5:13–14).

Strangely enough, there seems to be very little emphasis on singing in the New Testament. This makes me wonder how significant a part of their life it was. The only reference to singing in Acts, for example, is Acts 16:25–26, which is the account of Paul and Silas in prison.

What alarmed me here was that this solitary reference does not occur in a public meeting but in prison. If you had asked me for a synopsis of what the first believers did, I would have given you what I considered a synopsis of Acts 2: They met in the temple and then went to homes, sang songs, prayed, broke bread and ate together. All of that is true, except the singing bit. I was surprised to find that I had always added the singing part, because I always assumed it was there – maybe because that is what we have always done?[1]

Paul and Silas knew hymns and so must have sung them but, interestingly, Luke did not seem to think that it was significant enough to mention it as part of the gatherings of the early church whereas eating was!

There is only one mention of Jesus singing in the Gospels, although the same incident is mentioned in two of them (Matthew 26:30; Mark 14:26). This was after the last supper when they all "sang a hymn" and then left for Gethsemane. If

Jesus is the lens through which we interpret all Scripture, then the fact that there is only one mention of him singing should cause us to think.[2]

This was an uncomfortable revelation to me. Music had been one of the things dearest to me for years. I had played in a band for years and played in student events, pubs and clubs. That band had become oriented towards worship and we had recorded our own CDs and taught others in the whole area. I had written twenty or more songs that we had been singing over the years. Now here I was, looking at the Bible and seeing that what I had essentially built as the central activity of our church was relatively peripheral to the life of Jesus and the early church if we go by explicit references.[3]

The Greek word for worship used throughout the New Testament is *proskuneo*, which literally means to "prostrate oneself" or to "pay homage to", and is best summed up in the idea of a puppy at his master's feet. The concept was a familiar one at the time and would have described the way a loyal subject would respond to royalty or to an important person. There is a degree of adoration, love and intimacy in the understanding of this concept.

It is also significant that the word rarely appears outside the Gospels and Revelation – Paul only uses the word *once* – and that almost all the references throughout the New Testament are literal. In other words, whenever you see that word, it refers to someone actually bowing down or prostrating himself or herself, in most cases before Jesus. There is nothing there to suggest that they were singing to him.

Rethinking

I had always used this word with the assumption that it meant singing and then used this to denote intimacy and adoration in song. However, when I removed this assumption and looked at the example of a puppy at his master's feet, I began to wonder if the meaning actually has more to do with obedience. Whatever it did mean specifically, one thing that was increasingly and rather uncomfortably becoming clear was that it is not a metaphor for intimate songs. It is a description of someone falling on his or her face like a dog looking up at his master waiting for the next instruction. That is *proskuneo* – to sit at our master's feet, setting aside our agenda, waiting for his command.

I had made a leap of interpretation from a word that means a physical act of "bowing down" or "prostrating oneself" to saying that it means "singing songs". There is no doubt that Jesus, the disciples, the early church and the New Testament writers would all have assumed singing was a part of this concept but I think it is also fair to say that they never saw it as being exclusively, or even predominantly, so. Having read "singing" into every time the word *proskuneo* appeared, it is then easy to come to the conclusion that singing songs was the central act of the church. At best, this is a very dubious theological interpretation. In reality, it seems to have very little basis in the New Testament and so, surely, we have to ask some questions about this.

What can we conclude about worship?

As we look at singing in the New Testament, we see three notable things about the practice. First, singing does seem to have played some part in church life; second, singing is never equated with worship; third, while it is part of church life, singing does not seem to have been a particularly significant part of church life or Jesus' life, if the Gospels and Luke's accounts of the early church are to be taken seriously.

So, putting it all together, we have a church that met together every day, ate, apparently, on occasion, sang a few songs to each other and to God and served the poor, the lost and each other. We have to conclude that singing songs was a small part of what they did. The more I looked into it, the more I saw that the inevitable conclusion was that the New Testament church understood worship as including singing songs, but it was part of their overall worship, which embraced caring for one another, the poor and the lost.

I certainly believe that worship is our highest calling as believers. We would then have to agree that, if singing songs is all that worship is, this should take the bulk of our time, energy and money. We should employ people to write songs, to lead the music; we should invest as much as possible in training songwriters, singers, musicians and "worship" leaders; we should spread the word and encourage others to do the same. This was certainly my rationale until the rug was pulled out from under me. If, however, there is much more to biblical worship than merely singing songs, we need to think again.

As I looked at this I had to come to the conclusion that there are some key questions that we need to ask ourselves.

a. Have we taught people that singing songs is all that worship is?

I had always taught that worship is not just singing songs but is also about lifestyle but as I look back, I seriously question whether this message was really heard. In fact, as I have confessed, I do not think that I even heard it! I would go further and say that where I had referred to singing songs as "worship", it had been damaging.

I had to question what I communicated through my actions because, no matter how much I told people that it was not just singing, what I actually did – investing time, energy and money into music – communicated that worship was all about singing songs. One of the most popular songs in the Vineyard, and in similar churches over recent years, has been "Come, Now Is the Time to Worship", which is almost always used as an opening song. What does this communicate? It implies very clearly that the "worship" starts at the beginning of singing songs. Whether this was ever what was intended or not, I do not know, but that is how it is frequently used. Maybe we should only sing that song at the end of the meeting as everyone is leaving.

b. Have we set up a theology that actually discourages worship as a lifestyle?

The whole Vineyard theology of worship, which I have taught so many times, is built around the idea of a journey, drawing people, with a "call to worship", from a place of distance from God into intimacy with him. This, by definition, assumes that people have had a hard week and need to be drawn out of their "unholy" mindset into a "holy" mindset and intimacy with God. So, where I was trying to teach people to worship God every moment of every day, I was still arranging our "worship" with the assumption that they needed "charging up". Have we not set up a system that not only encourages, but also further exacerbates the "feed me" mentality?

I fully accept that focused time with God is important and that we do need space away from distractions to build our relationship with him. My observation was, however, that this was being done on Sundays for half an hour of singing instead of people actually building a relationship with him in their own lives.

This seems to be so opposite to the New Testament model and the early church's idea of people worshipping all week and coming together to encourage each other. It seems to me that what we have is perilously close to being a system designed to produce Christians who struggle through their week and survive long enough to be recharged on Sunday.

c. Have we set up an expectation of entertainment?

We worked hard at producing high quality music and so we had very stringent requirements of our musicians in order to produce what we called excellence. People were excluded from our bands because they were not good enough as musicians or because the instrument they played was just not cool enough. It was no good trying to fit flutes and trombones into funky, Indie rock music.

Ironically, the New Testament model is one where everyone comes and brings something to the meeting. As I looked around our church, I realised that the better the band was, the more exclusive we became and the more we discouraged other people from bringing anything. We had set up and reinforced the idea of the professionals at the front, which I would have claimed, repeatedly, we did not agree with. Also, the better we became, the more entertaining it was and the more we encouraged dependence on the professionals to feed the people. Over and over I tried to release people, but at the same time I was undermining it by modelling the opposite.

Rethinking

d. Do our songs reflect a New Testament emphasis?

Stuart Murray Williams has questioned the emphasis on individualistic ("I" and "me") songs in the church today. If we look at all the songs and prayers in the New Testament, we find that almost all of them are communal or just about God. There are very few that are individual. Jesus even tells us to go off on our own and pray the Lord's prayer, and yet we are still told to pray "Our Father".

As I looked at the songs that we were singing, I found that we had almost the opposite proportion to the New Testament – mainly songs that are personal prayers with a few exceptions. Our songs from the previous five years were very revealing. Around one hundred and seventy of them were completely individualistic, fewer than twenty were about the ways and character of God and fewer than six were communal.

The problem is that we live in a very individualistic society and I think that our songs have been driven more by that culture than by a healthy view of the Bible. The subjects of many of our songs are "me", "my faith", "my intentions" or "my desires". The whole emphasis of the New Testament is on us being a community and so all the prayers and songs should be about "we" (if they are about us at all!). We are not a group of individuals; we are the body of Christ joining together and singing as one.

I have also come to question the theology in many of the songs that we use. There is a prevalence of songs that talk about things being fine when we are "in God's presence". The New Testament teaches us that we are always in God's presence. A lot of popular songs ask the Holy Spirit to come, but the New Testament teaches that he is in us. There are times, clearly, when we experience the Holy Spirit moving powerfully but we need to be careful that we are not teaching that this can only happen in meetings or when we are singing songs. I will talk more about the idea of God being "present" in meetings in a later chapter.

The response may be that this is the language of the psalms to which I would pose this question – is that the teaching of the New Testament? Under the new convenant things have changed – certainly that does not invalidate the Old Testament but it does fulfil it. When David wrote his songs, Pentecost was just a twinkle in the eye of God. If Jesus is the fulfilment of the Old Testament, then he is the one through whom we should seek to understand and interpret it.

We teach far more through our songs than perhaps any other medium. Graham Cray has said that one can tell what a church or movement believes by their songbook. He also commented on the *Soul Survivor* songbook, which has a similar emphasis to that of the Vineyard, saying that there were "gaping holes" in the theology. As I looked at our own songbooks, I could not see many songs about the humanity of Christ, the sovereignty of God, his creation, the poor, his heart for the lost or his plan for the world. I understand that this was an attempt to redress a balance, but perhaps we have gone too far in the opposite direction.

As John Wimber noted, people will forget sermons but will always remember songs. Whether we mean to or not, we will communicate something and it is vital that what we communicate is consistent with what the Bible teaches. My fear is that we are actually communicating a very small part of the gospel, plus some erroneous theology, as well as the individualism of our society, namely that the only goal of our faith is we, as individuals, each seeking to further our own personal relationship with God.

e. Does it matter?

What scares me most, as I said at the beginning of the chapter, is reading the Old Testament prophets and seeing a frightening parallel between Israel and the church: "But Lord, have we not sung our songs to you ...?" (See Isaiah 58 and Amos 5, to name a couple.) If we call "songs", "worship", then people come on a Sunday and sing and think that they have "worshipped" and fulfilled their Christian responsibility. But this is not what the Bible refers to as worship and God is fairly clear, through Amos, about what he thought about that: "I hate it, take your horrible songs away!" The worrying thing was that because the Israelites were meeting and singing their songs and having their feasts and festivals, they thought that they were worshipping God.

I think that understanding what worship really is does matter. This is not just semantics. I am genuinely trying to work out how we respond to our highest calling. Is that to sing songs, or is it to seek to become radical disciples, building radical churches, that are impacting communities with the way that we worship God, day in and day out?

Notes

1. The New Testament believers did attend temple worship (Acts 2:46, 3:1–10) and did meet in synagogues (Acts 6:9), and since both involved singing, we can infer a practice of singing in the early church.

2. Jesus did include singing in his description of the celebration for the return of the prodigal son (Luke 15:25). We can infer, therefore, that Jesus viewed singing as included in the kind of celebration that results from a new-found faith.

3. Since our knowledge of the historical Jesus is through the eyes of the Gospel writers, we can never assume that we have an exhaustive knowledge of how he lived. Since he was a first-century Jew, one can infer that he may have been as involved in singing as most people were in that society. One could also argue that, since the Gospels do witness to his continual confrontation with the religious leaders and practices of the day and never recall Jesus explicitly naming singing as a symptom of their dead spirituality, he was not unhappy with the contemporary practices in regard to singing.

8

Leading, Serving and Toilet Cleaning

I'm not just saying it to make you feel better

Is it just me who sins? How come everyone else is so holy? How on earth am I ever going to live up to the lives of these great men and women of God that I hear speaking from the platform, "encouraging" and exhorting me? Please do not misunderstand me, the stories of what God has done are amazing and really do encourage me. The thing is that I cannot help feeling as though that will never happen to me, because I am never going to be perfect and free from all temptations like these people. I suppose I am always just going to be a second-class Christian.

I remember my youth minister taking me with him on a trip. I think that it was to the Oasis Trust in London but I have no memory of why. I was a new Christian – I would have been about nineteen and I had not long ago been to Spring Harvest. Spring Harvest is a large, residential Christian conference held at several sites (normally Butlins holiday camps) across the UK during the Easter holidays. Virtually all of our church went along to one week or another of this every year because our minister was one of the main organisers of the event. I vividly recall sitting on the train and saying how much I had enjoyed the whole thing. I did not know there were so many Christians in this country! It was fantastic and God did some amazing things. Then I remember saying words to the effect of, "It would have been so much better if these guys (the speakers) would say 'God did this through me or for me or to me *but I was still struggling with this or with that area of my life'*, because it would give me so much more hope for myself!"

I was then, and I am now, a pretty wretched Christian all in all. I struggle with pride and selfishness and any number of other things. Anyone who knows me well will vouch for these things – especially my wife, who has no illusions about my "godliness". What she would tell you is that, among other things, I really need to sort out my problem with anger. And she is right. It's better than it used to be but compared with Jesus, or even with her, that is not really great. I am moving forward and being transformed, I am making progress, but I have not completely dealt with it. I am sure that a large part of my problem with anger comes from the fact that I am always right and so, when others do not agree, there is an issue. Some people just do not seem to appreciate the burden of omniscience. So, there we have it – pride, as well.

At the time of writing this (December 2002), I am in Zimbabwe on sabbatical. I have heard myself expressing my various opinions, and believe me, I have an opinion on everything, unless I am not aware of its existence. I do really believe these opinions –

especially about the poor, obedience and lifestyle – but then I look in the mirror and I have to admit how bad I am at actually doing what I say. I am trying – most of the time – I really am. I really do not want to be like that, but the truth is that I am.

The point is, I am not infallible. Actually, I am about as fallible as it gets! Paul puts it really well:

> I know I am rotten through and through so far as my old sinful nature is concerned. No matter which way I turn, I can't make myself do right. I want to, but I can't. When I want to do good, I don't. And when I try not to do wrong, I do it anyway. (Romans 7:18–19)

We read that and we know that Paul was just saying that to make us feel better and actually he was perfect and never struggled with sin in his life. It is as though he is throwing out a little token just to keep us interested. Either that or Paul was a human being too and actually did struggle with the same temptations that we do. Now there is a radical thought! I suppose that the option that he really did mean it is a possibility.

I am not sure we really believe that. I wonder whether the culture of churches is, maybe, too much that the pastor/vicar/minister/leader/elder/person at the front is some great holy and infallible pseudo-human. In moments of frustration with our church, I am sometimes tempted to wonder if, perhaps, it would be good for me to cultivate that impression, and then people might stop questioning things that I say and do.

Without doubt we, as leaders, need to be modelling what we teach, but are people not much more likely to follow someone who is transparent and humble because they can relate to them?

Rethinking

What are we trying to model anyway: deception or truth? Do we want communities full of people pretending to be doing really well when their lives are a shambles? Did Jesus not absolutely lay into the Pharisees for that very thing (Matthew 23)? Surely we want our communities to be made up of people who are open, honest and transparent. In other words, "sharing their lives in common", which is what the Greek word for "fellowship" (*koinoinia*) actually means.

Here I was, a new Christian, a sinner by all accounts, yet really wanting to serve God and wanting him to use me. All I seemed to be hearing was perfect preachers with perfect lives talking about their perfect ministries. All the other Christians I knew were perfect and I was the only one struggling, so I never admitted to anyone that I was struggling. What hope was there for someone like me to move on and to change? I was stuffed! I could only conclude that there was no hope for someone like me.

The first time I heard John Wimber speak, I could not believe it. A friend had lent me a pirate copy (okay, I confess, forgive me – I was not the one who recorded it though!) of a conference from America. John Wimber was the leader of the Vineyard movement. Actually, I had read his book, *Power Evangelism*, some years earlier (in fact, it was the first Christian book I had ever read) and it had really affected me. Hearing him speak was a similar experience. Here was someone who was talking about the amazing things God had done through him and for him and to him and talking about his own shortcomings and failures and struggles. I had found someone who was speaking in a way that I had always hoped leaders would. I had found something that I could commit to: honesty, integrity and transparency.

Obviously, I didn't really believe that he struggled with anything, but I did appreciate the fact that he had made the effort to pretend to have some weaknesses in order to make me feel better. It was only years later when I was speaking myself, as I was talking about my own failings and weaknesses, that it hit me like a bolt of revelation. He was not lying. He really meant it! It was the truth! I was sounding like him! What else can I do? Surely it is a far heavier burden to bear to pretend to be a perfect saint when I am clearly not? I would never get away with it! Surely it is easier to admit to weakness?

It was actually this that first attracted me to the Vineyard as a movement. For most it is the music but for me it was the openness and transparency. I loved it. I loved being able to relate to someone and feel that what they do or are is really attainable for me. I am really not very good at being encouraged by someone who is out of my reach. I tend to give up. I love waterskiing, but when I see someone who is really good, I want to give up and start playing golf. When I see someone who is similar to me or who is a little bit better than me, I can be challenged and feel as though we are in this together and we can help one another to move forward.

Is anyone actually following?

There are two words in the New Testament for authority. One *authentio*, is only used once (2 Timothy 2:12) and has the connotations of usurping authority, tyranny and "taking by force". It is even used in the Septuagint (the Greek translation of the Old Testament) to describe a wild animal ravaging another animal. The whole understanding is one of grasping authority for ourselves. The other word, *exousia*, is by far the most used and has the clear understanding of authority being given as opposed to taken. The sense is that this is given, by those that you lead, as well as by God. Your responsibility is actually to work that out.

John Wimber used to say that if no one is following you, you are clearly not a leader – whatever your title or "official" position. The other side of this coin is that if you are a leader, people will always follow you – whether you like it or not, whether you have a title or not. According to Roland Allen in *Missonary Methods: St Paul's or Ours*, Paul, in his missionary work, had a way of working that is alien to most of our church culture. He led many to Christ, moved on to the next town, and the next and then, after a while, revisited all the churches and appointed leaders (Acts 14:21–23). He waited to see who the leaders actually were before he appointed them. This is also reflected in his advice to Timothy (1 Timothy 5:17–22) not to be hasty in the laying on of hands, the context being what to look for when appointing leaders and laying hands on them to affirm authority.

I used to think that it was some kind of achievement to be a leader or that leaders were something special. Many of the churches and denominations that I have come across seem to encourage this view through clothing, titles or expected behaviour. There are so many people in our church who are far godlier than I. I just happened to have been given the job of leading.

We are all in this together

We are one body. We are meant to be working together for the good of that body because the combining of all of these parts is a beautiful thing that reflects the glory of our Saviour. Each of us has a part to play in this that no one else can play and I believe that a pastor is just one of these parts. I believe that no one part is more important than the other.

> But God made our bodies with many parts, and he has put each part just where he wants it. (1 Corinthians 12:18)

My understanding of this passage is that, while I may (or may not) be great at being a toenail of the left little toe of the body of Christ, that certainly does not make me any better than your role as an excellent right nostril. We are all in this together for the communal good. We are all trying to help one another towards Christlikeness and all that I can do is to be obedient to him and be that part in the body that he made me to be, playing my role with that aim. What else can I do?

> Faith in Christ Jesus is what makes each of you equal with each other, whether you are Jew or Greek or slave or a free person, a man or a woman. (Galatians 3:28, CEV)

Earlier in the same passage, Paul has talked about how slaves should behave with respect to their masters. Is he contradicting himself only a couple of sentences later by saying that there is no difference? Not at all. He is clear that there are different roles and he is absolutely clear that role has nothing to do with value in Jesus' economy.

I have played silly games with children on visits to India, tickling, being tickled, dancing and having fun, and then found the same children, an hour later, when they discovered that I was a pastor, bowing down in front of me wanting me to pray for them because I am a "great man of God". It made me want to weep. I had gone out of my way to be childlike and normal and then been presented with a false pedestal that I did not want to stand on.

One of my friends in our church told me something that made me laugh. Just before our holiday last year, one of the people in our church was facing a situation that was potentially very serious. This person had spoken to our friend and proclaimed that it was going to be okay "because Matt's praying for us". She responded in her inimitable fashion with, "Matt's not praying for you. Matt's waterskiing in Greece. We're the one's who are here praying for you!" She was right. Why would my prayers be any more powerful than hers, or than her 18-month-old daughter's, for that matter?

Being see-through nobodies

I committed myself to the value of being transparent as a leader. I do not know any other way of doing it. I am not smart enough to get away with pretending to be holier than that and not stupid enough to think that I am anything more than a left little-toenail, so I have to.

Someone asked me recently how I would challenge a congregation about an issue – in this case I think that it was pride – without antagonising them. Well, I specialise in a bulldozer-like ability to get people's backs up. Fortunately, I married Di, who has an amazing ability to go around behind me clearing up the mess and repairing the damage! So I may not have been the best person to ask. However, I told them that I would just use myself as the example of struggling. There is no subject that I can speak on that I do not struggle with myself, so I would just be honest about my own weaknesses. I would say how God has challenged me and is continuing to challenge me in that area. I do not think that this is rocket science, but it did seem like an entirely new concept to this person.

How does that happen? How can we think that we need to present a faultless front? We are all human, so no one, least of all God, is going to fall for it. It is the old classic cliché: "When you point your finger, you have three more fingers pointing back at you." So do not point your finger unless you are willing to admit that you are a prime example of the problem.

Paul calls his readers to imitate him (1 Corinthians 4:16). How better than to imitate the genuine working through and ultimate victory over sin that he, as all of us, has gone through and, in our case, are still going through. We are all in this together. We all want to be like Christ. We are all equal. We are all struggling with sin. So let us be "church" as it should be – a community helping one another to "work out our salvation". A community of transparent people, truly living our lives together with no superstars. That is a good starting point.

Community or career?

I have never really been able to get my head around the idea that anyone could see pastoral ministry as a career. I just cannot work out how anyone could intentionally commit themselves to one group of people for a short time knowing that when a better opportunity arises, they will leave. I do accept that, on occasion, God may call someone to another community, but I cannot conceive how one could lead a church intending to leave after a given time.

Rethinking

Church is about relationship with Christ and one another, from my reading of the New Testament, and surely we want authentic "community" – a word that, distressingly, is becoming more and more trendy and less and less meaningful in church circles. If we want this, how can anyone see this as a career step? Leaders are there to serve our community, not so that our community can serve our career. (Knowing God's sense of humour, I'll probably get called to another church somewhere and then I'll have to apologise to everyone I have offended by saying this!)

What I find frightening about this is that it seems to echo our society's fear of real commitment. To put it very crudely, it sounds much more like the self-gratifying approach of a one-night stand than the lifetime commitment to work through a relationship. Maybe this is not such a crude illustration when we look at Paul's criteria for leaders in his letter to Timothy.

"What about Paul?" I hear you say. Well, he was an "apostle" – a sent one. It would seem that the very role of an apostle in the New Testament was to start a ministry, a work or a community, and then appoint leaders. He clearly saw the role of a church leader as being distinct from his own as an apostle. He must have been very lonely. When he writes to Timothy giving him criteria for choosing leaders (1 Timothy 3:1–12), he uses family life and marriage as his benchmark. Surely there is nothing more permanent and committed that he could have used to make the point.

> If anyone does not know how to manage his own family, how can he take care of God's church? (1 Timothy 3:5, NIV)

In marriage, God's way, the option to just up and leave because you prefer someone else's family or wife is not really there. Does Exodus not say something about that (Exodus 20)?

I do believe that God may and does call people away, but that is different to just getting a better offer. I cannot imagine leaving our church. I really intend to be in this for the long run. These are my friends, my family, the ones with whom I want to live my life. If I did ever leave, I cannot imagine someone from the outside coming in and taking over from me. It is about real relationship and that comes before titles or position.

Serving the community

Where am I going with this? Well, basically, leadership is servanthood (John 13; Matthew 20:25–28; Mark 10:42–45; Luke 22:25–30). It is a responsibility to serve a community of people who are striving to serve Jesus and to be the people that he created them to be in his great story, and that is a terrifying responsibility. If you think that status comes with this, you are barking up the wrong tree. I believe with all my heart that there is absolutely no room for ambition in Christian leadership.

> Jesus called them together and said, "You know that the rulers of the Gentiles lord it over them, and their high officials exercise authority over them. Not so with you. Instead, whoever wants to become great among you must be your servant. (Matthew 20:25–26, NIV)

God needed to change a great deal in me before I was ever going to lead. Maybe I was always a leader but as long as my heart was full of ambition and a desire to be "seen", it was never going to happen. (That is, assuming that God loves his church enough to not damage it irreparably by letting me loose on it!) I am not saying that I do not still struggle with ambition and pride, because I do. Rarely a Sunday goes by without me wanting to impress people. But I have changed and, thank God, am still being changed. I want to see this community, this group of people, my friends, my family, walking in obedience to Christ, serving the poor and loving the world as Christ does. I want to do whatever I can to facilitate that process. That is what I am about now.

Paul said of Timothy that he was "distracted with cares" for the people that he served in Philippi (Philippians 2:20). What I understand from this is that he lay in bed at night unable to sleep because of the concern that he felt about the things that some of them did, with the worry for their well being, the joy of the things going well, the fear of hurting people or messing up and the desperate desire to do what is right for these people. His heart would have sunk when he knew about the foolish choices that people had made. Very few moments went by when he was not thinking about them or how best to communicate what God had put on his heart for them. The mistakes that he had made would have stuck in his mind for years. When one of them was angry or upset with him, it would have cut so deeply that it may have taken years to heal – or maybe it never did.

That is my experience, and it may well be that after reading this you feel that I need psychological help. I cannot believe that anyone would sign up for this because they think that it would, in some way, make them look "cool". Paul sarcastically described himself and the other apostles as the "scum of the earth" (1 Corinthians 4:9–13). This, by the way, is an extremely polite translation for what dogs leave behind in the park!

Leading, Serving and Toilet Cleaning

Leadership is the bottom of the pile, not the top. There are two things I would want to know in choosing a leader. The first, as mentioned earlier, is whether anyone is actually following them. The second is whether he or she is a servant. Do they do the washing up? Do they clear up? Do they run around giving people lifts? Do they do the jobs that no one else wants to do?

We recently decided that we would do our own cleaning in our office – the two pastors and the administrator. It's not much – the toilet and kitchen, the dusting and the vacuuming. How easy it is to have too many "important" things to do that make cleaning the toilet impossible. If you cannot clean a toilet, you do not know what servant leadership means. Washing feet in the first century was roughly the equivalent of cleaning toilets today.

Jesus' whole life was a model of what leadership actually means. He served from start to finish, he loved and committed himself to those he led and he embodied everything that he taught. I once heard Rich Nathan, a Vineyard pastor from Columbus, Ohio say that the secret of leadership was "to lead". No great revelation, you may think, but in reality most leaders do not "lead", they "point".

Section III

REDESIGNING

9

MESSING UP THE CHURCH

The systems you have ...

What defines a church? I do not know anymore. Certainly not meetings; surely not structure; it could not be size; absolutely not a building. When is a group of Jesus' disciples a church? When is a ministry a church? When is parachurch church? I do not know. If church means "a group of like-minded people" – and that is what the New Testament Greek word *ecclesia*, which we translate "church", means – then we need to think. For example, an organisation ministering to the poor, made up of half a dozen people committed to serving Christ in this way, working together five or six days a week, praying together and, in reality, living their lives together, sounds a lot more like church than many of the "churches" that I have seen. In fact, it sounds quite a lot like Acts 2 and Acts 4 to me.

What if our definition of church is actually a hindrance to the kingdom of God and not a help? What if we started from scratch, setting aside our assumptions and prejudice, and saw what we came up with? Or could it be that our structures – and

Redesigning

I am not just talking about traditional churches – have become more important than the purpose that they were originally set up to serve?

Todd Hunter has been possibly the biggest single influence on me as he has tied much of the thinking around this issue together and sought to work it out in a church/community setting. When he quoted a well-known business adage "the systems that you have are perfectly designed to produce the results you are getting", I realised that things would need to change. If we have a church that is full of half-committed people, then it is not despite what we do, but precisely because of it. Looking at the church in the UK, which is shrinking at an alarming rate, and comparing it with the church in the developing world, we must ask some questions!

I realised that our own church was built around a system of persuading people to pray a prayer and then, basically, entertaining them and trying to meet some of their needs, until they die. That may be slightly simplistic, or even harsh, and I am sure that there are exceptions but, in the main we were not geared up to raise disciples – people whose lives are totally characterised by Christlikeness – but rather to make converts. The New Testament has no concept of a convert who is not a disciple. How did we end up with a lesser definition of Christianity? Real, radical discipleship has become something for the elite minority in our churches whereas, in the New Testament it is the only option; it is what defines you as a believer. We were not teaching people to be like Jesus but just getting them to "cross the line" so that they will be okay when they die.

I have spent the last few years messing up our church as I have

Messing Up the Church

tried to address this, attempting to become a church that is built around making disciples. It has been painful and I have nearly given the whole thing up on several occasions, but God has not let me. I went to a conference in California and challenged God that if he did not speak clearly and directly to me – through an unknowing third person – by the end of the week, I was going to find a "proper" job! As it happened God, in his infinite patience, put up with me throwing my toys out of the pram and indulged me by providing that very person. That person was, in fact, John Mumford, the National Director of the Vineyard in the UK, who just happened to be in California and just happened to pop in for one session and, just as he was leaving, prophesied all this stuff over me. The fact that it was John was probably significant as he is the one in authority over us in the Vineyard. Okay, God, you win!

As I said in a previous chapter, I realised that we had set up a system whereby people came to a meeting on a Sunday where we, in some way, "recharged" them, enabling them to survive the week in the big bad world. What I saw in the New Testament, however, was a system whereby people worshipped and interacted with God seven days a week and then came together out of that worship to encourage one another. The difference is between "come and be fed" and "come and feed one another". In my mind, we had to find a way to release people to be dependent on their own time and relationship with Christ rather than our meetings. This is not an easy thing to do. I, for one, had to change my whole way of thinking and that inevitably meant changing my life!

However hard it was – and it was really hard, and in many ways still is – and however much easier it would be just to go back to the way that it was, I could not do it. As a pastor said to me recently, "I just could not go back to what we had before because, even if this is not the right thing, I know that that isn't."

Blowing up the temple

Basically, we set about decentralising everything that we could. We got rid of the professionals and the entertainment, and we have tried to teach and model that worship is what happens throughout the week. We have tried to make the meetings the place where people can all come and bring, as opposed to just receiving. The emphasis is on being a community, living lives of worship, and not on putting on great meetings to substitute for the relationship with Jesus that was lacking in people's lives.

It was hard, because many people do not want to be put into the position where their lives are, in a sense, under the scrutiny of the rest of the family. If you come to a meeting where you are only asked to sit back and be entertained, no one knows what is really going on with your life – as demonstrated by my own life – but if you have to contribute, you are vulnerable. On the other hand, some (not all) of the professionals (the musicians) did not want to be taken out of the spotlight and one needs to ask why that might be.

There is no question that in many ways our meetings are not as slick, well-presented or entertaining as they used to be. The band is gone and so the standard of musicianship varies from week to week. There is not music every week, but when there is, many of those involved are nervous and not always great at what they are doing – but so what?

In practice, what we did was to place all the housegroups – and our church is built around these groups, so being part of the church means being in one of these – on a rota to lead the first half of each meeting. This way, everyone in the church has a chance to contribute to the main meetings. People may read poetry they have written or that has touched them, tell their story, lead communion or invite people to be involved in creating a picture. Or they may just lead us in singing songs.

I'll tell you what, though, there are some gifted people with exciting stories to tell that I never knew were there, who would never have been given the freedom of expression before. Apart from them being encouraged and released as a result, I am convinced that the church would have been poorer without their gifts.

Most exciting for me is that I am beginning to see disciples who are beginning to walk a life of worship – day in, day out – who come to encourage one another and learn to be family together. One person said to me that they have found it hard over the time that we have been doing this, but they have realised that they are only in the place they are in with God now because of it. Ironically, another person complained that they were having to spend more time with God regularly to compensate for this shift in emphasis! The whole criteria for our meetings have changed. No longer am I looking for a great event at which people feel great and are topped up and entertained. Instead, I am looking at the meeting to see evidence of discipleship of the people in our church and the outworking of their daily worship.

In my experience, until we radically changed our meetings, nothing actually changed. I think that the root of the problem is that most of us view Sunday meetings as "the temple" – the place where we meet God. This, I am afraid, is clearly shown by the way that we spend time, energy and money on these meetings. How do we justify the idea that we meet God in Sunday meetings? Is Bitterne Park Junior School where God lives? Are we, the people of God, not the house of God (1 Peter 2:5; Ephesians 2:19–22)? Is Jesus not the temple (John 2:20–22) – the place where God and man meet? Surely a large reason that we struggle to find disciples in our churches is that we have taught and modelled that God lives in our meetings and that our meetings are the high points of our experience with God. Think about the implications of that. The average church in the United States spends eighty-five percent of its income on its Sunday meetings. The New Testament church – and the church that followed for the next two hundred and fifty years – spent nearly all of its income on the poor and needy. Can you spot the difference?

While I taught that worship was a lifestyle, yet continued to model something different, i.e. that Sunday meetings were the main focus, nothing changed. When we changed the Sunday meetings, requiring everyone to contribute to them, many of the people in our church were not happy. To be honest, I did rather pull the rug out from everyone's feet and so it is not surprising that people were slightly confused and more than a little put out. The fact was, though, that I had had the rug pulled out from under my feet. As I waded through the complaints and arguments, the real problems became more and more obvious.

Firstly, a number of people did not like the fact that they were not being entertained anymore. Here is a question that bears serious thought. How can the "standard" of the "worship" be set by how good the musicians are? What is good worship? Does it mean how good it feels to us? Surely, looking at the whole of Scripture, we can see that what God sees as good worship is, in fact, the way that we live our lives. Do we really believe that he is more interested in musicianship than our lives? Maybe what we have experienced and called good worship has little to do with God and more to do with us. Now there is something to think about!

Secondly, many people did not like the idea that the onus was on them to pursue a relationship with Jesus rather than us, the corporate "church", to provide it for them. What became alarmingly clear was that a large proportion of our church had very little, or no, relationship with God other than what we provided them with on Sundays and at housegroup meetings. As long as we continued to provide it, they did not need to do anything about it.

I used the following example on one occasion to explain what has happened to our meetings. Before, everyone came along and we gave them a big feast. Now, everyone comes along with their picnic basket full of the things that they have put in during the week, and we all share our food together. If your basket is empty, then people will know and they can help you to be able to fill it for next time. The point is that what is eaten is what has been brought along. The whole emphasis is on your life with Christ that week.

This may sound shocking and even extreme, but I really mean it – I really do not care what actually happens at our meetings, as long as it is encouraging. I really, really care how people are

Redesigning

working out their lives together and with Jesus.

If I am honest, I look back and there are many aspects of what we used to have that I miss. I miss playing in the band and I miss the music. The thing is though, at the end of this age, I am going to stand before God. It is my guess that he is not going to say this, "Your church did not care about the poor, they had no real relationship with me, and they were unconcerned about the lost; but, hey, I loved your meetings. Well done, good and faithful servant!" It just does not sound quite right, does it?

I promise you that, as a pastor, when you start to mess with the emphasis on Sunday meetings, you will be left in a very insecure and vulnerable place. What is your role? What is church? You have fifteen hundred years of church history to examine. You have a lot of prejudice to work through. You may even find that you have a far smaller role than you had before. You certainly have less control. You may find that people begin to get on with working out their faith as a community and your part in this is just to oversee the church and help people to work out their own vision and calling. It is scary and I am still working through my role in all of this. I think that I still have one, but I know that it is very different from what it was before.

It is a scary thing to mess with your meetings like this and there are many reasons why I am reluctant to recommend it. I do not think that it is possible to grow a big church this way. In fact, it is very likely that you may lose people in the process and that will mean that you have a smaller church than you started with. As well as the issues of credibility that are involved in shrinking a church, there are the obvious financial implications, which I suspect, if you are a pastor, may well be higher on your list of priorities than you would like them to be. Also, people may think that you are a cult or slightly weird. This whole process is, without doubt, not one to boast about at leaders' conferences. You do not often hear people saying things like, "Yeah, numbers are down, income is down. The church is in great shape!"

What I have experienced with our church has led me to believe that unless you are willing to blow up the misconceived temple, things will not change. I taught on worship being about lifestyle for nearly two years and everyone could pretty much repeat it back to me. It was not until we messed up our Sundays that it became clear that no one had actually believed what I had said, and I do include myself in that. As long as I could get "blessed" on Sunday, I could get away without really pursuing a relationship with Jesus myself. I am ashamed to say it, but it is true. Changing Sunday meetings forced me into having to spend more time with Jesus.

We visited the Church of the Saviour in Washington, DC. a few years ago and spent several days there. I have absolutely no idea what their church services are like. I do, however, have a pretty good idea what they are like as a community. The two overriding emphases of this church were the "inward journey" – cultivating a deep and real relationship with Jesus through disciplines and devotion – and the "outward journey" – ministering to the poor and the hopeless, the sick and the socially and economically excluded around them. To me, that sounds like a church that has its priorities sorted out. I was challenged that this is what "church" is – a group of people seeking to serve God together. It hit me that if you had asked me to describe our church to you at that time, I would probably just have described a meeting.

Redesigning

Meetings or church?

Somehow, the idea of a weekly meeting has replaced real fellowship – by which I mean "holding our lives in common" as opposed to a cup of instant coffee and a few superficial clichés. We call a weekly meeting "church". We talk about "going to church". How can you go to church? You are the church! In many places, arguably, church has ceased to be a dynamic representation of Christ on earth, reaching out to the community and serving the poor, and has become not much more than a weekly meeting. As I said earlier, I do not know what church should look like, although I have one or two ideas. I am convinced, however, that its essence has nothing to do with buildings, meetings or preachers and everything to do with a group of disciples spurring one another on to a closer intimacy with Christ and a greater walk following him.

There are a host of things about our church that are not the way that I would want them. Some, but not all, of this is because we have had to turn the ship around and people – me included – have had to relearn many things. I love our church but we are on a journey and, frankly, we are just starting out. I know that my life does not match up to the kind of life that I would want it to be and so it comes as no surprise that our church does not match up to the kind of church that I would want it to be. I have to start to address the problem somewhere and I reckon that the best place to start is with me.

I was asked recently what I would do differently if I were planting a church again. I did not have to think for long because I have been thinking about little else recently. My reply was that I would start with a blank sheet of paper and I would set out my objectives. They would be something like building a community of believers who are released to be the people that God called them to be, who genuinely and deeply know, love and serve Christ and one another and who serve the poor and the outcasts as part of their normal lives.

I would then write on my blank sheet of paper the best ways to accomplish each of those things. I would have to get rid of all my assumptions about what church "should" be like in order to do this. I know for sure that the answers I would come up with would look very little like what we assume is normal church.

A few years ago I was involved in a forum with a group of young leaders from Vineyards across the country, all of whom were involved in leading "alternative" services within larger churches. We asked the question: If you could start with a blank sheet of paper, how would you go about creating family, an army, school and hospital. John Wimber described these categories as, in essence, what the local church is.

People wrote down their thoughts on post-its and stuck them onto the flipchart, over a period of fifteen minutes or so. The results were shocking. Literally, not one thing that anyone had put up there corresponded to, or could be achieved by, what they were actually doing. If every one of us had started with a blank sheet of paper, none of us would have done things the way that we have.

We have so many assumptions about what church actually is, that we rarely entertain any questions outside these very narrow borders. Often, what is called "radical" is merely a different style of music, a different venue or using different

Redesigning

language, but is still well and truly within those accepted parameters. Maybe we need to stop tinkering with the aesthetics and actually take a long, hard look at the basic expectations of how we are church which, I believe, are not only not helpful in accomplishing our mission, but are actually counterproductive.

The systems you have are perfectly designed to produce the results you are getting.

10

REBUILDING THE CHURCH

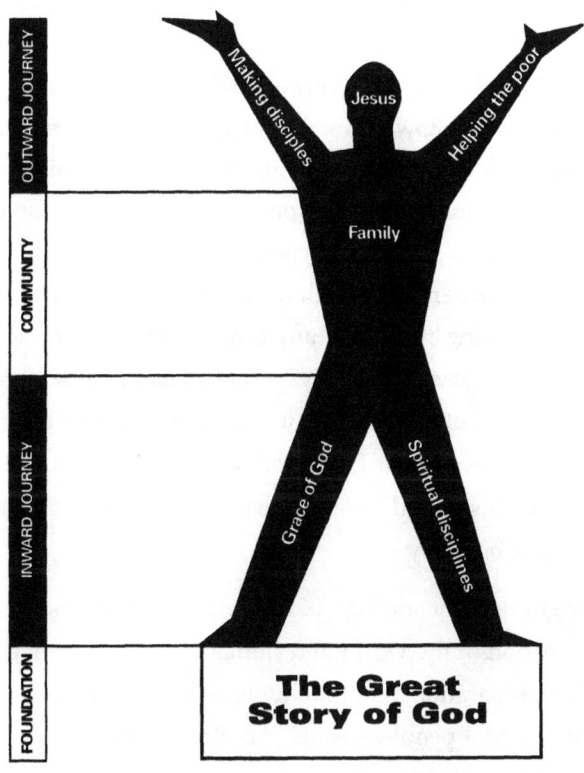

The Southampton Vineyard Person

Redesigning

This is Southampton Vineyard Person. It is an adaptation of "Vineyard Man" that John Wimber used as a graphic representation of the Vineyard movement. This is different in that it is a representation of a single church – our church, to be specific – rather than a whole movement. This represents who we are and what we are about as a local church. I will explain the Southampton Vineyard Person. in this chapter.

The foundation

There is a great story unfolding – his story (history – I wonder if that is deliberate?). It is interesting to note that only religions based on the Bible have any concept of linear time – time coming from and working towards something. All the other religions of the world have a cyclic view of time. In the Chinese calendar, for example, there are sixty years – one person's lifespan – and then they begin again and the cycle continues. Are we living as though we are part of something or are we just existing in a cyclic way, trying not to do anything wrong but not actually seeking to engage with the story? So often I find myself forgetting that we are part of this overarching plan, and become caught up in going nowhere, then I wonder why I lack vision. I do not believe that this is God's plan for us. According to the Bible, we are part of a big story.

NT Wright uses the analogy of a play to describe this. Act One is the creation of the world and humanity in God's image. Act Two is the separation of humanity from God. Act Three is God's covenant with a people – Israel. Act Four is the coming of the one that his people have waited for – the Messiah, Jesus. Act Five, however, is for us to act out ourselves. We have only the first scene and some of the author's notes on the ending. We must improvise the final act. We can only do this if we are so familiar with the author and how he works that we can anticipate how he would have written it. We must also know the story so well that we will automatically act in harmony with it, until it culminates with Jesus' return, the end of this age and the beginning of the age to come.

As Todd Hunter has reminded me on several occasions, each morning we wake up in the middle of a story that is already unfolding. Each of us is uniquely gifted, placed, experienced and called to play our part in that story. There can be no substitute for knowing the author and the story so well that our part is natural because there is no script. Only by each one of us being freed to be the person that God created us to be can we play that part. Only by each of us playing our part can the church be what it should be.

To put it another way, each one of us is a player in a football team. We bring our skills and our gifts to the team. If the goalkeeper decides that, because he can kick a football, he may as well be the striker, the team will suffer. Our unique gifts mean that no one else can fulfil the role that we play as well as we can. For us to opt out or not seek to pursue or develop our gifts, or to try to fit in somewhere other than our role, means that the team will be the worse for it. If, however, we learn to help each other to become the person that we were created to be, we will have a strong, effective team who compliment each other perfectly.

It is my belief that every single one of us is "called". Often that word has only been applied to those in "ministry" or those called to "mission". We are all called to ministry and we are all called to mission. God may have called you to be an accountant and to minister the way that Jesus would in that field. He may have called you to be a lawyer, a doctor, a social worker, an IT analyst or even a pastor. The point is that each of us is called to be the kind of person that Jesus would be in that role and in the place where we are, day by day.

Look at it another way. Each of us is a diamond in a diamond necklace. There may be two hundred diamonds but if one were missing, it would be broken. Each one of those precious gems is beautiful in its own right but the combined beauty of the whole necklace is far greater. We each have a place in the necklace that no one else can fill, and if we will find our place, the beauty will be a stunning offering to our Saviour!

Finding and living out our part in this great story is the foundation of who we are as a church.

Inward journey

This language, as I have mentioned, is taken from the Church of the Saviour in Washington, DC. The whole concept is that our journey is a pursuit of a deep, personal relationship with Jesus. We can easily become drawn into doing stuff and not really know him. We can prophesy in his name, cast out demons in his name, feed the poor, put out the chairs, play in the worship band, and then be shocked when he says, "I never *knew* you" (Matthew 7:21–23 NIV, my italic). It is easy for us to read that passage and write it off as being for those who just sit in traditional churches and do not participate. Not so, read it again!

> Not all people who sound religious are really godly. They may refer to me as 'Lord', but they still won't enter the Kingdom of Heaven. The decisive issue is whether they obey my Father in heaven. On judgement day many will tell me, 'Lord, Lord, we prophesied in your name and cast out demons in your name and performed many miracles in your name.' But I will reply, 'I never knew you. Go away; the things you did were unauthorised.' (Matthew 7:21-23)

How can we know the story without knowing the author? How can we know him unless we cultivate a real, deep relationship with him through prayer, Bible study, listening and communing (that is a good Christian word) with him? How can I say that I have a relationship with my wife if I never spend time with her? Surely the definition of relationship is spending time with someone, communicating on some level. How can I say that I have a relationship with Jesus if I never spend time with him? This is our inward journey. These are "the legs" on which our church stands – the relationship that each of our people has with their Saviour. There are two legs – the grace of God and spiritual disciplines.

I have said a lot so far about the way God has spoken to me and worked on my conscience. I have shared my frequent feelings of guilt. I want to clarify that the way I have struggled with guilt is not my message, or even my understanding of the biblical message. It is just my struggle, no more and no less. It is important to say again: The Christian life is not supposed to be a life of guilt, but one of joy. Please do not hear this confession of my struggles as some form of legalism or that I do not believe in the incredible grace of God.

The grace of God

We are saved by grace (Ephesians 2:8–9; Romans 3:24). As I said before, I do not believe that salvation is merely about what happens to us when we die, but that we are saved from a wasted existence and saved to real life. Not because of us, not because we deserve it, but because God took the initiative and reached out to us. Jesus died for us. He paid our price, once and for all. There is nothing more to pay. He shows us how to live and if we believe (trust) in him, we are saved. It is he who leads us through this life and helps us to become more like him. We cannot earn this. He loves us. He just does! I need his grace to live day by day because, without him guiding me, strengthening me, enabling me and gifting me, I would fall and never recover.

When I teach people how to waterski, I have always been aware that every step of the learning process is a letting go of your natural instincts and trusting the instructor and the boat. The first thing that happens when you feel the pull of the boat is that your body says, "Stand up" or "Pull yourself up". Either of those options will leave you swimming – one of them face down with skis floating away and the other with the skis still on but floating on your back. To learn to ski means that you need to let go of your agenda and actually trust what you have been told. If you do that, you will ski on top of the water.

On the whole the Protestant church, especially house churches, has been pretty good at emphasising grace, largely (and rightly) as a reaction to legalism. Often I have heard grace used like a "get out of jail" card. Sadly, I have watched Christians, who have chosen to live their own way and not obey God, respond to any correction by saying that it is all "covered by grace".

In other words, I can live however I want to and God will just let it go. This, to my mind, is a serious misunderstanding of what God has for us. We cannot waterski if we try to do things our way. That is not legalism, it is just fact. God wants us to be free. He does not want us to be bound or addicted to the things that the world tells us are good, because that is not really living. He does not want us to be floating in the water with our skis floating down the lake because that is not skiing. He wants us to be free to really live, and the only way that we can do that is to let go of the things that stop us from being truly alive.

We have to trust him. We cannot do it our way. The boat is more than 300 h.p.; it can pull you up. You, on the other hand, cannot, even if you are the strongest man in the world. You need that boat to be able to ski. Unfortunately, doing nothing in that situation is a very active thing. It takes a lot of concentration to continue to trust. Once you are actually up and skiing, you are still dependent on the boat. This is not the time to take over with your own plan, because no matter what level of waterskier you are, you still need to continue to let go of your agenda and to trust. You need to look at the boat and not the water and you need to relax and not try to make things happen.

This is grace. We need that grace because we cannot do it ourselves. We need to continue to trust in Jesus and his continuing grace for us. We need to accept that the power of the boat is not against us but actually for us, and the only thing that enables us to continue. It is the power of God and his continuing love for us that enables us to continue living. He is for us.

Accepting God's love for us is not an easy thing – for some of us it may even need to be a discipline. Our past, our upbringing, our self-image, our experiences all shape the assumptions that we have about God and the way he relates to us. In many cases, a lot of healing needs to take place before we are secure enough in the grace of God to put our weight on this leg.

I know how sinful I am. I know that I really do not deserve this love. Every day I have to ask for forgiveness. Actually, it is more like every half-an-hour! I hate the sin in me and I know that it sometimes takes me ages to forgive myself – much longer, ironically, than it takes the very one against whom I have sinned – God himself. It paralyses me or, as the writer to the Hebrews puts it (Hebrews 12), "it *so* easily entangles" me. The solution, from the same author, is to "fix our eyes on Jesus". This may be easier said than done but it is still the answer.

Church should be a place where the grace of God is overwhelming; a community where love is the overriding factor; where it is clear that people are for one another; a community where God's love for his children is demonstrated, day in, day out. Sadly, in many places the church has a reputation for the opposite. The story at the beginning of Philip Yancey's book, *What's so Amazing About Grace*, is a stark reminder. When a prostitute, who was desperate for help, was asked if she had ever thought of going to church, her reply was, "Why would I ever go there? I was already feeling terrible about myself …"

God just loves you. He knows what you are like and he still loves you! This is the starting point of our entire walk with him. We cannot trust him unless we first trust that he is for us. He loves us so much that he offers us life – free. If we try to earn it, we will never be free. We just have to accept it. It would take the rest of my life to repay the financial and emotional debt that I owe my parents for the first twenty or so years of my life. I would just never be free of it. They do not ask me to repay them but rather accept it as the place from which to build my life. How are you going to repay God? You just cannot. Start there, knowing that he is for you, that he loves you and that you really can trust him and live your life in freedom.

The spiritual disciplines

Just the phrase "spiritual disciplines" is likely to make most of us who are Protestants very nervous. Certainly that was how I felt and consequently I would keep as far away as possible from any book that contained the word "disciplines" in its title. I have come to realise and indeed experience that spiritual disciplines are actually a way to freedom.

Disciplines are merely a scaffolding to help us to build change into our lives. They are not the building itself. The aim of disciplines is to reach the point where we no longer need disciplines. Apparently it takes about six weeks for a habit to form, or to be broken. When something becomes a habit, it is no longer a discipline. For me, reading my Bible was a difficulty and so I set myself a reading schedule and forced myself to read my Bible regularly until, over time, it became a habit and I could actually not do without it.

"Grace" does not mean that we have no part to play. We are free because of God's grace, but unless we work out that freedom, we will cease to be free. We cannot earn God's love, but that does not mean that we can walk with him without effort. Paul urges us to "run the race to win" and to "beat our bodies into submission" (1 Corithians 9:24–27), to "work out our salvation" (Philippians 2:12). Peter tells us to "make every effort to add to" our salvation (2 Peter 1:5–9). The writer to the Hebrews tells us to "run with perseverance the race marked out before us" (Hebrews 12:1–3). All of these are very much *doing* and *effort* exhortations. But were we not just talking about being saved by grace?

If I took the grace that my parents showed me in underwriting the first eighteen years of my life, and then chose to do nothing, is that living? How can I, knowing that I can trust Jesus, choose not to trust him? Trusting him means trusting that what he says is true; that how he lived is the way to live and that obeying him is the way to be free.

We are saved by grace, but saved from what? From a wasted existence that will leave us dead. Jesus has demonstrated the way to live freely. We have this freedom available to us, if we will trust him and work it out. Working it out is not a legal requirement; it is just the way that we are free. We cannot continue to walk in the opposite direction to him and still be following him – that is a contradiction in terms! Learning to follow him is not a natural thing. Allowing him to change us so that it becomes the natural thing is where we have to make every effort to train ourselves to work out our salvation.

We have been given the gift of life. The Holy Spirit lives in us. Unless we learn to work that out, we will never appreciate this gift. We will always be frustrated because we have not learned to build a life like Jesus – the kind of life that we are designed to live – and we keep waiting for it just to happen to us.

> The general human failing is that we want what is right and important, but at the same time not to commit ourselves to the kind of life that will produce the kind of action we know to be right and the condition we want to enjoy. (Dallas Willard, *The Spirit of the Disciplines*)

What are spiritual disciplines? Imagine that I am really bad at reading my Bible. A good discipline for me would be to commit myself to read my Bible three times a week or to read a book of the Bible in a week or a fortnight, until reading the Bible becomes a habit. Or imagine that I am great with people, but really not good at being on my own. A good discipline for me would be to start to spend five minutes each day on my own in silence until I become comfortable with solitude and silence. Maybe I am very comfortable on my own but cannot cope with people. A good discipline for me would be to spend time with others until I am comfortable with it. Perhaps I need to look at my lifestyle and I need to question how much time I spend in front of the TV, playing on the PlayStation, how much money I give away, or whatever.

As we slowly seek to order our lives, so that God is allowed to work in us, we find that we begin to live the life that we have been given. It is hard work changing the habits of a lifetime but we have the Spirit of God living in us and enabling us to do so. The day I reach the point that I no longer need disciplines is the day that Jesus has returned! Some of my friends think that I am a very disciplined person. Yeah, right! The very reason that I have to take on so many disciplines is because, by nature, I am not at all disciplined. These range from eating five items of fruit and vegetables a day and not drinking more than three cups of coffee a day, to reading the Bible through each year, keeping a spiritual journal and being still before God for a certain amount of time each day. Some of these things have become a habit; others are still a bit more of a battle.

Ultimately, I want to be like Jesus. Jesus' life was built on regular, committed time alone with his Father, listening to him and obeying him. On this foundation was built his ministry and from it flowed his power. I need to work on a whole life like Jesus and not just the "get away from me Satan", "be healed", "see" and "stand up and walk" bits. As I work on building my relationship with Christ, the "stand up and be healed" bit comes a bit more naturally.

Outward journey

The arms on the figure on p. 135 are reaching out. Jesus was very clear that he has a mission (Luke 4:18–19) and it did not end when he died. This mission continues today, and Jesus chooses to use us, his church, for this. Basically, we have been assigned this mission and it is a non-negotiable. Making disciples is not just the job of the "professionals". If we are following Jesus, we need to go where he is going and it is fairly clear where that is. Ministry to the poor is not just the job of the half-dozen people who do the soup run every week. It is all of our jobs.

While there is suffering, injustice, poverty and people who are destitute, it is our "mission", as followers of Jesus, to do all that we can do to address it. Simple. If we think that this is not the case, I am afraid that there are an awful lot of parts of the Bible that we need to remove! Much of the judgement on Israel that led to exile was because they stopped doing this (Isaiah 58; Ezekiel 16:48–52; Amos 5, etc.).

God's rule – his Kingdom – is coming, and it is here. God is at work healing the sick, raising the dead, casting out demons and setting the captives free. That is our work. The story of the talents (Matthew 25:14–30) should be a fairly clear pointer as to what is expected of us. As I said elsewhere, I was the king of Pharisees when I was a new Christian (I am still pretty high ranking now) and I had the view that being a Christian was all about trying not to do anything wrong. "I don't sleep around, I don't get drunk, I don't lie, I don't speed … I buried my coin so that nothing bad could happen to it." We have a mission and it is not to be fixated with the things that we should not be doing. We need to realise that God has made us to go out into the world and to be his hands.

I would love to say that I model what it is to follow Jesus in his mission – and maybe, on the odd good day if you caught me at exactly the right moment, I do. I would love to be an example of how to love the unlovely and those who are excluded but I am ultimately very selfish. I would love to say that I am the best neighbour that anyone could have but that is not true. Actually, my other next-door neighbour (who is not a Christian) brings us food from his allotment, looks after our pets, knows everyone in our street, puts out everyone's bins for them, does occasional building jobs for our church and generally, in that respect, is more like Jesus than we are. I would love to say the poor are flocking in and the sick are being healed and that the city of Southampton is radically different because of us, but I would have to lie to do that.

Redesigning

I am constantly asking God to help me become the kind of person who does follow Jesus into his mission field. I, like many others, read stories like that of Jackie Pullinger and I am inspired but I also feel guilty – mainly because I am guilty! I really want to have the kind of love that will override my nice, middle-class barriers. Like it or not, one day we will be asked what we did with our talents and I do not think that "I buried it" will be the answer that Jesus was looking for.

Making disciples

> Therefore, go and make disciples of all nations, baptising them in the name of the Father and the Son and the Holy Spirit. (Matthew 28:19, NIV)

Not "evangelism"; not "converting" people; not getting people to "pray this prayer", but making disciples – showing people Christ – through our lives, loving them like Christ loves them and helping them to follow him and realise their life in him. This is committing ourselves to those around us so that they can know what it means to have real life.

Someone once asked me, "Do you love your friends enough to want to see them become Christians or do you just want them to become Christians so much that you will love them in order to accomplish this?" The point is, do we really care about those around us or are they just a project? We need to be as Jesus to those around us. I have to say that I am rubbish at this – my wife, on the other hand, is absolutely fantastic at it. I need to work at it. It is not an option for me not to.

If I reached one person this year and they became a disciple, then next year we each made one disciple, the next year the four of us go out and do the same, etc. In twenty-five years, the whole population of the UK will be followers of Jesus. I know that all I can do is just a drop in the ocean, but the ocean is made of drops.

In all the time our church has been in existence, I can honestly say that I know of no one who has become a disciple through an event. It was always through relationships. They may have started following Christ at an event, but the fact is that they only came to an event because of a relationship. Everyone that I know has become a disciple because they saw something in the lives of the people here and saw that there was something missing in their own lives. Most of them saw a love in the church that they had never experienced before. I think Jesus said something about that (John 13:35).

Love people, show them Jesus and let them see in you what they do not have. It may take a long time, but what else do you have to do? When we were at university, I watched all of Di's friends as they got drunk or stoned around her, as they went through various boyfriends and girlfriends and as they mocked her faith. Then I watched them come to her, one by one, as their lives began to crumble, and say, "You have your life sorted out. I don't know anyone else like that so I thought I could talk to you."

I have to admit that I was too busy trying to win arguments to really love people. Making sure that they knew that they were wrong was more important to me than showing them Jesus. You know, there are a few places in Acts where the apostles try to argue out their faith – in Jerusalem (Acts 9:28–29; 21:37–22:29;

23:1–10); in Athens (Acts 17:22–34); Paul before Felix and Agrippa (Acts 24:10–27; 26:1–32). The results stand in stark contrast with the results of all the other missionary attempts. In these cases very few were saved, whereas the language of the other is "many", "more" and "all" (Acts 2:43–47; 5:12–14; 8:6–12; 9:39–43).

Loving people is hard. Especially when they are hard to love and particluarly when you are a bombastic idiot like me. I remember being at a wedding some years ago and getting into an argument with the husband of one of Di's closest friends who was not a Christian. We were both really angry at the end of it and it literally took years for all our relationships to be healed. For years after it happened, I was still convinced that I had been serving Jesus in what I had done. I would say, "I hope that he finds out that he is wrong before he dies." This guy is a doctor, at the time in his mid-twenties, and had devoted himself to working with AIDS victims. I look back now and I realise that, even though he was not a Christian, maybe, in some areas, he had a better handle on what it meant to follow Jesus than I did. What he objected to was the black and whiteness of the church and bigoted Christians like me. I have a lot to learn from him.

People are not projects. They are children of God who he desperately loves and he hates to see their lives wasted and heading for the cosmic rubbish dump. How much do we love them? How much do we want them to be free from addiction? Enough to commit our lives to serving them and loving them and basically, being Jesus to them? The main thing standing between the world and Jesus is the church. If people do not want to know Jesus, it is because of what they see in the church.

Rebuilding the Church

The point I am making is that we are the body of Christ (1 Corinthians 12; 2 Corinthians 4:10–11; Ephesians 1:22–23; 3:6; 4; 5:22–23, 30; Philippians 1:20; Colossians 1:18, 24; 3:15). We are also described as being built as God's building (Ephesians 2:19–22) with overtones of the temple, the place where God and Humanity met; the place where the Gentiles could come to seek him. Just the idea that we, the church, come in the name of Christ and are ambassadors of Christ (2 Corinthians 5:20), means that we have a responsibility to represent Christ accurately. An ambassador speaks on behalf of the one who sent him. If that ambassador acts badly, what he does affects the image of the one who sent him. Combining these concepts, we have to realise that we are his image to the world and the world judges who Christ is and what he is like from what they see in the church. Therefore, when they see something that does not actually reflect him, we are actually standing between them and him in a negative way and not, as we should be, reflecting him to them so that people see the real Jesus. We need to work that one through because I, for one, am really not a great advertisement for Jesus.

Ministering to the poor

> But when the Son of Man comes in his glory, and all the angels with him, then he will sit upon his glorious throne. All the nations will be gathered in his presence, and he will separate them as a shepherd separates the sheep from the goats. He will place the sheep at his right hand and the goats at his left. Then the King will say to those on the right, 'Come, you who are blessed by my

Father, inherit the Kingdom prepared for you from the foundation of the world. For I was hungry, and you fed me. I was thirsty, and you gave me a drink. I was a stranger, and you invited me into your home. I was naked, and you gave me clothing. I was sick, and you cared for me. I was in prison, and you visited me.'

Then these righteous ones will reply, 'Lord, when did we ever see you hungry and feed you? Or thirsty and give you something to drink? Or a stranger and show you hospitality? Or naked and give you clothing? When did we ever see you sick or in prison, and visit you?' And the King will tell them, 'I assure you, when you did it to one of the least of these my brothers and sisters, you were doing it to me!'

Then the King will turn to those on the left and say, 'Away with you, you cursed ones, into the eternal fire prepared for the Devil and his demons! For I was hungry, and you didn't feed me. I was thirsty, and you didn't give me anything to drink. I was a stranger, and you didn't invite me into your home. I was naked, and you gave me no clothing. I was sick and in prison, and you didn't visit me.'

Then they will reply, 'Lord, when did we ever see you hungry or thirsty or a stranger or naked or sick or in prison, and not help you?' And he will answer, 'I assure you, when you refused to help the least of these my brothers and sisters, you were refusing to help me.' And they will go away into eternal punishment, but the righteous will go into eternal life. (Matthew 25:31–46)

Rebuilding the Church

I think that this is one of the scariest passages in the whole of Scripture. God separates the sheep from the goats on the basis of how they responded (or not) to the poor. Think about that! How does that fit in with our theology of "pray that prayer and go to heaven when we die"?

Just think about the implications of this.

> We have to become aware that the poor are the hope of humanity, for we will be judged on how we treated the poor. (Mother Teresa, *No Greater Love*)

Helping the poor is such an integral part of what it means to follow Jesus that we will be judged on it. I do not know about you, but that really frightens me when I look at the church in the UK and when I look at my own life. We do not have the option of ignoring the poor. We just cannot afford to. Serving the poor, in my view, is as much part of being a Christian as praying and reading the Bible.

I have never been taught anything about this, in any church that I have been part of. At best, there has seemed to be a small handful of members who do something with soup every so often, but I have never heard that it is part of my discipleship. If the gospel is good news to the poor, why is the church in the West almost exclusively middle class? Perhaps the gospel we preach is not good news for the poor, in which case we need to re-examine it.

I mentioned this earlier, but I do still think that it is valid. I also understand how someone living in Africa can think that this is ridiculous! I met an English woman in Zimbabwe. Her husband had travelled a lot through his work to many developing countries and she had accompanied him. She told me that the poorest people she had ever seen were about two blocks behind the White House in Washington DC.

As Wimber used to say frequently, "You can tell what people value from their cheque book stubs." The church in Acts gave virtually all its money to the poor, both in and outside the church. This was the case for the first two hundred and fifty years of the church's history. In fact, according to Stuart Murray Williams (*Beyond Tithing*), helping the poor was one of the primary forms of outreach of the early church. He goes on to trace the change. With the advent of Christendom, within the space of about eighty years, the church's money went from most being given to the poor, to being divided between the poor, the clergy and the buildings, to being divided between the clergy, the buildings and the bishop. Has it changed very much since then? How many churches give even ten percent to the poor? I was told about an "incredibly generous" church that aimed to give twenty percent away. By today's standards this is extremely good, but whose standards are we being judged by?

The poor are not easy to reach. To be honest, it can be very hard work, very unrewarding and can cost us a great deal. When a couple from our church took in a homeless guy, serving him and loving him and being Jesus to him, he racked up a large bill on their credit card, stole a load of stuff from them, stole their neighbour's car and disappeared. We have other, similar friends whom we hardly ever hear from unless they want money, a lift or a bed. When we stop jumping every time they want us to, they disappear. Sometimes we become frustrated because these people do not "get saved", but that is not the point. It is our role to serve them whether or not they ever give their lives to Jesus. Just because it is the right thing to do!

Community

The inward journey and the outward journey are worked out in community. The individualism of Western Society is not a biblical concept. Fellowship does not mean a few superficial pleasantries before or after a service. It literally means "holding our lives in common". It means being accountable to each other – over our time, our money, our values, our priorities, our secret lives, our sin, our weaknesses, our strengths, our joys, our fears, etc. It means having the permission to challenge each other about anything. It means helping each other out so that there are no needy people among us. It means really caring for each other and really preferring one another's needs. It means being a shoulder to cry on. It means looking out for each other and truly demonstrating agape love. It is this unique love that should characterise us, by which the world will see Jesus among us. That is what I mean by community because that is my understanding of what the Bible means by community.

I need help to be more disciplined and so I need others, who are for me and with me, who will help me to do that. I need help because I do not naturally hang out with the poor and so I need others, who are for me and with me, who will hold me to account over this and help me to do this. I need to confess my sin and to be changed into the kind of person who will not sin. I need those around me whom I can trust implicitly, who love me and who are for me and with me, to hear my confession and help me to change. When my heart is broken, I need someone who is for me and with me, who has a shoulder that I can cry on. When I am happy, I need people who are for me and with me to share that joy. Have you ever tried watching a really funny comedy on your own – it is just not the same!. When I am learning to prophesy, to pray for people or to grow in faith, I need people around me who are for me and with me who will not laugh at me when I make mistakes.

When we were in South Africa, we had the privilege of going on safari. We spent much of that time trying to see the most widespread but most elusive of Africa's big cats, the leopard. Apparently one of the leopard's favourite foods is baboon. Now the baboon is no match for the leopard, but the leopard rarely manages to eat his favourite food because baboons stick very close together. In fact, a troop of baboons is a formidable force and have been known literally to tear leopards apart. The only chance the leopard has is to pick on a baboon that is on the fringes of the troop where is not protected by being part of the community. "The devil prowls around like a roaring [leopard]" (1 Peter 5:8, NIV). We are like a troop of baboons.

We need to be part of a community that will help one another to become the people that they were made to be. We need to be part of a community that is seeking to be the body that will find and take its part in this great story. We were just not made to do this on our own. Working out our inward journey is not possible for us unless we have people spurring us on. Working out our outward journey is not possible without others helping us to do it.

Humans seem to be very much like chameleons, I find. If you hang around with people who are materialistic, you find yourself becoming more and more so. Recently we had a meal with friends. These friends are extremely rich, as are most of their friends. The topic of conversation among the men quickly got onto coping with the unreliability of your Ferrari or Lotus, or why one needs to replace one's BMW with a Range Rover. I found myself wanting to say things that would enable me to fit in, but somehow, "Yeah, my Peugeot Diesel has great fuel consumption," just did not seem to cut it. I just could not help but want to fit in; it is in our nature. Back with the people of my church, this conversation seems absurd. Why on earth would I want to try to impress people with lots of money with my first-hand knowledge of supercars (not that I actually have any first-hand knowledge of supercars, but I can play along!)?

If we hang out with those who value simple lifestyles and godliness, we find it easier to pursue these things. In many ways, that is what church is – or should be – a group of people rubbing up against one another and challenging each other to further godliness by example.

I am lazy, I am selfish, I am greedy, I am sinful and, on bad days, I am even worse. If it were not for the people around me who constantly challenge and encourage me, I would more than likely be heading off in totally the wrong direction. I need these people more than they need me. I have to be accountable to them for my time with God, my Bible study, my sin, what I have done with my time and money and whether I have been with the poor, among other things. Because I have to be accountable to them, I have a chance to correct things before I have to be accountable to God.

Our whole Western culture is one of individualism, and the idea of letting others into your life is alien to us. If you do not think so, ask someone in your church how much money he or she earns. What does that have to do with you? That is my business! If we hold our lives in common, I am not sure that anything is just "my business" anymore. If I am not willing to be called to account, then we are not in community. While it is really painful and extremely hard, we have to lose this cultural addiction to individualism. Interestingly, very few of the prayers in the New Testament use "me" language. There are around six hundred prayers, according to John Wimber, and what I was amazed to discover was that almost all of them use "we" language. Even in the Lord's prayer (Matthew 6:9–13) when Jesus exhorts us to go off on our own, he still teaches us to pray "our Father".

No one is saying that it is easy. The more you open up to people, the more vulnerable you will be and the more they can really hurt you. There have been times in the history of this church when people have hurt us desperately. Maybe it would not have hurt so much if we had not been so close in the first place. Sometimes people can be extremely unpleasant – I know that I can. But however hard it is to love one another, we are one body. We need each other. We just will not be able to become like Jesus unless we do this together. Like it or not, it is the case. As Wimber used to say, "I love the bridegroom, but have you seen the bride!"

The head

Christ is the head of the church (Ephesians 5:23) and I sincerely hope that he is also the head of our little, local church. Frankly, if Jesus is not the head of this church, maybe we need to pack up and go home. If the Holy Spirit is not the one guiding us, we really do not have much of a chance. As soon as this becomes my church, we are in trouble because this is his church and I just have a role within that body. He does not need me to do it but he does, very graciously, let me participate and risk me messing up his beloved bride.

It is all about him. It is not about us. It is for his glory and not for ours. It is not about my agenda but his. He has a different set of values to ours. Ultimately, it does not really matter what anyone else thinks, because it is him whom we are serving. That is hard for me to walk out. Of course I care what people think of me. Taking risks is scary if you end up looking stupid. Being able to say that I am living before "an audience of one" is freeing indeed. It is amazing to know that we have to give an account only to him.

We can only do the best we can to serve him. These chapters are our latest best guess on how to do this. I will be the first to hold up my hand and admit that we are not there yet. I do not know whether we will ever become what we are aiming for before Jesus returns or we come up with another plan. I do know that I desperately want to be part of a community of people who really love one another, really know Jesus, really make disciples, really serve the oppressed and the poor, and know their place in this great story.

I am not suggesting that this is the only way. Obviously, if I did not think it was the best thing for us, I would not do it. I do believe that we have to ask some questions. I do believe that we need to think seriously about the fruit of our churches. We can easily get stuck in a groove that is comfortable and never really question whether it is right. That would certainly be the easiest thing for me to do. Most weeks I think to myself that it would be so much simpler just to go back to the way it was. We could get back to having great meetings, we could grow a big church and I could be comfortable and, in many ways, successful. It is a frightening thought that, of the seven churches in Revelation (Revelation 2–3), the two that received unreserved criticism (Sardis and Laodicea) were the two largest, wealthiest, most "successful" churches. Jesus describes Sardis as being dead and to Laodicea he says that he is not even in the church but standing outside trying to get in! Can you imagine receiving that kind of rebuke from Jesus?

I know that the day that we stop questioning what we do and just settle for "this is the way that we have always done it" is the day that we are in trouble. Messing up our church has been painful for me. I meet a lot of people in different settings who are seeking some kind of "new" expression of church because they are disenchanted with church as they have known it. This was not the way that it was for me. In fact, I loved the way it was, but I knew that I just could not leave things the way they were when I did not believe in them anymore. I had to make changes, whatever the cost, because I know that one day I will stand before Jesus and I will have to give account of my life and how I oversaw this little community that he left me to look after. I want, more than anything in my life, to hear him say, "Well done, good and faithful servant." It is that single thing that gets me out of bed and drives me on every moment of every day.

BOOKS I HAVE FOUND HELPFUL

These are all readable books that are not too academic. They have helped to shape my questions over recent years. If you want to pursue this, these are books you may want to look out for. I have selected the ones that I have found most accessible, that have had the most impact on me.

Steve Chalk and Alan Mann, *The Lost Message of Jesus*, Zondervan, 2003

This is a fantastically easy to read book. It summarises much of what NT Wright and Dallas Willard say in a very readable way. If you do not fancy working through either of the above authors then this is the book to read. Brilliant!

Stuart Murray, *Beyond Tithing*, Paternoster Press, 2000

This book made me completely rethink "church"; how we spend our time, energy and money and how we impact the poor. This is a challenging book and really affected my lifestyle, so beware!

Stuart Murray, *Post Christendom*, Paternoster Press, 2004

This book works through the changes that Christendom brought to the church and causes us to question many of our basic assumptions. Stuart's teaching on this is what started me on the whole journey of rethinking. That may be a recommendation or a warning to you!

Books I Have Found Helpful

Christopher Rowland, *Revelation*, Epworth Press, 1993

This book is a commentary on Revelation. When I eventually sat down to study this book that hides at the back of the Bible (despite me trying to ignore it), I found it to be the most exciting book in the New Testament and I now find myself reading the whole Bible in the light of it. Chris's book was not only instrumental in this but it really excited me and challenged me in terms of values and lifestyle. It is not a long book and it is very readable. You might, however, have difficulty getting hold of it.

Dallas Willard, *The Divine Conspiracy*, Fount, 1998

Now here's a book that ruined my life. It challenged me to rethink my understanding of what it means to be "saved". It can be quite hard work to read but it really is worth it. I can honestly say that virtually everyone I know who has read it has been profoundly affected and said that it changed their life.

Dallas Willard, *The Spirit of the Disciplines*, Hodder & Stoughton, 1988

This is a much easier book to read than *The Divine Conspiracy* and really helped me to understand how to build the spiritual disciplines into my life. More than this, it was the first time that I actually saw the disciplines as the way to freedom rather than as a burden, and that was revolutionary for me.

NT Wright, *The Challenge of Jesus*, SPCK, 2000

This book really challenged me about my mistaken assumptions about who Jesus actually was and is, helped me to build a more accurate picture both biblically and historically, and to understand better the context into which he ministered. If we want to follow him it is vital to know who we are following.

NT Wright, *Following Jesus*, SPCK, 1998

I have found this to be one of the easiest of Tom Wright's books to read. It seems to encapsulate many of the things he speaks of in other books and it is less than one hundred pages long. If you only buy one of his books, get this one.

NT Wright, *The New Heavens and the New Earth*, Grove Books, 1999

This book is great. It is about twenty-five pages long and I think that this is the perfect length for a book! There is a lot of stuff out there about the end times and a lot of it seems to have a fairly dubious biblical basis. This book challenges a lot of the unbiblical assumptions about the end times and the age to come, building a biblical view which, frankly, made me reassess how I live.

Philip Yancey, *The Jesus I Never Knew*, Marshall Pickering, 1995

I found this so helpful in understanding the humanity of Jesus. We do not usually think of Jesus' humanity and often it makes us uncomfortable to do so. I think that we miss a lot of the point because of this. I was so excited reading this as it opened the door to a Jesus that I had somehow missed altogether. It is, like all of his books, very easy to read.

Philip Yancey, *Soul Survivor*, Hodder & Stoughton, 2001

I really enjoyed this book because, again, it made me rethink my assumptions and made me ask more questions. It is basically the stories of several different Christians who, in many cases, do not "fit" and yet serve or served Christ in radical ways. Some people I found easier to connect with than others and I am sure that this will be the same for everyone. Again, easy to read.

Books I Have Found Helpful

***The Good Shopping Guide*,** **Ethical Marketing Ltd, 2002**

A lot of people want to be ethically and environmentally conscious in how to buy and live but do not actually know where to start or what is good or bad. This is a reference book and covers items from TVs to banks, washing powder to perfume, insurance to toys and grades the different companies on environment, animal rights and human rights. If you are serious about thinking through your lifestyle in this respect, this book is an absolute must. It is available on the Internet from www.thegoodshoppingguide.co.uk.

www.ingramcontent.com/pod-product-compliance
Lightning Source LLC
Chambersburg PA
CBHW071433160426
43195CB00013B/1886